SECRETS OF BUSINESS DEVELOPMENT

··

TRUSTED ADVISOR CONFIDENTIAL

THE INSIDER'S GUIDE TO LANDING RIGHT-FIT CLIENTS

··

CRAIG LOWDER AND HENRY DEVRIES

INDIE BOOKS
INTERNATIONAL

ISBN-13: 978-1-957651-44-6
Library of Congress Control Number: 2023912822

Designed by Amit Dey

INDIE BOOKS INTERNATIONAL', INC.
2511 WOODLANDS WAY
OCEANSIDE, CA 92054

www.indiebooksintl.com

CONTENTS

PART I

Cracking The Code On Finding Qualified Prospects

1

Why Business Development Can Be A Mystery For Trusted Advisors

The fault is not in our stars, but in ourselves.

William Shakespeare, in *Julius Caesar*

No trusted advisor who has ridden the income roller coaster enjoys the ride.

An alternative is to get off the roller coaster and let the stars guide your business development efforts: six stars to be exact.

These six stars are what successful trusted advisors follow to guide their business development journey in pursuit of a sustainable book-of-business and personal income growth.

The biggest mystery for trusted advisors is how to attract increasing numbers of right-fit clients on a regular basis. In short, predictable and sustainable book-of-business growth.

The biggest mystery for trusted advisors is how to attract increasing numbers of right-fit clients on a regular basis. In short, predictable and sustainable book-of-business growth.

Ironically, many trusted advisors feel business development is too time-consuming, expensive, or undignified. Even if they do make a short-lived business development effort, most trusted advisors are frustrated by a lack of results. They even worry whether a sustained business development effort would ever work for them.

No wonder they are doubtful and worried. According to former Harvard Business School professor and author David Maister, the typical business development and marketing hype that works for retailers and manufacturers is not only a waste of time and money for trusted advisors, but it also actually makes them less attractive to prospective clients.[1]

But research has proven there is a better way. There are proven systems for business development with integrity that can generate up to 400 percent to 2,000 percent return on your investment.[2] This is the NavSTAR Client Acquisition System outlined in this book.

NavSTAR Client Acquisition System Strategy #8

The "People Buy From People" strategy: Even if there are twenty on the team, each trusted advisor must first sell themselves, not the firm. People do business with people they know, like, and trust.

All ideas in this book have been tested nationwide over the past thirty years by the two authors: Craig Lowder of Chicago and Henry DeVries of San Diego. They have been paid millions and millions of dollars for the advice contained in this slender volume.

The following trusted advisors from professional services firms were included in our research studies:

- Financial advisors
- Independent consultants and coaches
- Marketing and advertising agency owners

Not All Advisors Are Trusted Advisors

Being a trusted advisor means you are good at what you do. Nothing in this book will help you much if you are not good. If you do attract clients and cannot satisfy them, they will tell everyone they know to avoid you. And with the power of social media, that is a great deal of potential people they can tell.

However, just being good is not good enough. A reputation as a trusted advisor is a fine attribute; however, it will not produce the benefits of the NavSTAR Client Acquisition System.

There is a myth that if you do good work, then clients will find you. We two authors are here to debunk the good work myth. In California, we tell trusted advisors that the universe rewards activity; in the Midwest, we explain it as this: "The Lord helps those who help themselves."

NavSTAR Client Acquisition System Strategy #16

The "Plant Three Seeds A Day" strategy: There is a universal truth that as you sow, so shall you reap. A trusted advisor should plant at least three seeds each and every day to attract clients.

Stop The Income Roller Coaster, I Want To Get Off

What should you do if you are one of those trusted advisors who wants to exit the income roller coaster? First, understand that finding clients is an investment and should be measured like any other investment. Next, quit wasting money on ineffective means like brochures, advertising, and sponsorships. The best lead-generation investment you can make is to create informative websites, host persuasive seminars, book speaking engagements, and get regularly published as a blog columnist and eventually as the author of a book.

The details of a proven client acquisition system are illustrated in this book by true life stories like the following:

The Lisa Apolinski Story

In 2012, Lisa Apolinski quit the corporate grind to form her own digital marketing consulting agency. Apolinski is the founder and CEO of 3 Dog Write Inc., a full-service digital consulting agency. 3 Dog Write provides strategic consulting around digital engagement, content creation, and the proper use of digital assets.

To create an effective client acquisition system Apolinski has worked hard to become an international speaker. She is considered a digital engagement thought leader and has worked in the industry for more than two decades. In 2019 she added book author to her resume.

"A wise business today guards its digital assets like the United States guards the gold in Fort Knox," says Apolinski, author of the book *Weathering the Digital Storm: How to Fortify Your Digital Growth Strategies in Unpredictable Times.*

The book is leading to more speaking opportunities in front of target-rich environments of prospects. Apolinski speaks on digital growth strategies, which includes promotional outreach using digital technologies, mainly through the internet, but also including mobile phones and any other digital media.

"Digital marketing is like a climb with no summit," says Apolinski. "But this climb, while continuous and difficult at times, can bring insight, growth, and strength to your organization."

Top Three Reasons Your Book Of Business Is Not Growing As Expected

1. **You are not following a business development system that ensures a high level of lead conversion to paying client.** Without a documented lead-conversion process that mirrors your prospect's buying journey, you will never be able to build a solid book of business. Typically, successful, trusted advisors have a minimum of three lead-conversion processes they follow.

2. **You have not implemented a system and strategies for generating high-quality leads.** Without a system for determining your return on investment (ROI), there is a high likelihood that you are wasting your most precious resources: your time and money. Successful, trusted advisors generate quality leads from five to ten strategies.

3. **You have not established goals and a system for dedicating time to business development activities.** Without goals and a time-tracking system, you will never be able to reach your business development and income goals. Trusted advisors realize that time is perishable and must be managed wisely to achieve success.

2

Insider's Guide To Landing High-Paying Clients: Meet The NavSTAR Client Acquisition System

All I ask is a tall ship and a star to steer her by.

Poet John Masefield

Quit being reactive in your client acquisition efforts. Start being proactive.

A proactive system enables trusted advisors to generate a significant, predictable, and sustainable book of business. Proactive client acquisition can systematically produce results when applied correctly and managed scientifically.

The main message of this book is this: client acquisition is a science that must be artfully executed, especially by trusted advisors. Like any other science, there are scientific client acquisition principles to follow.

Much like in the field of medicine, there needs to be a diagnosis before a prescription. The diagnosis, while artfully detected, is based on a body of knowledge. After a prescription, there needs to be intense monitoring of the patient. In medicine, they call it the vital signs. In client acquisition, we call it the key performance indicators (KPIs).

Here is the good news. The dream of creating a client acquisition system that will generate significant, predictable, and sustainable book-of-business growth is obtainable; however, you must try to learn how other successful trusted advisors have done it and then apply that knowledge.

The Added Benefits

The primary benefit of adopting a proactive and systematic approach is to generate significant, predictable, and sustainable book-of-business growth. Here is a rundown of the other key benefits:

Shorter Client Acquisition Cycle. There is an adage in business development that time kills deals. The longer a deal takes to close, the less likely it will actually close. The NavSTAR Client Acquisition System seeks to close more deals by shortening the buying process.

Higher Lead-To-New-Client Conversion Rates. Leads are like at bats in baseball. Increasing your batting average means converting more of the leads into new clients. Small increases in conversion rates can have a huge impact on gross income and net personal income growth.

More Upselling And Cross-Selling Opportunities. The NavSTAR Client Acquisition System helps trusted advisors focus on the number of deals. Increasing the number of transactions can significantly affect gross income and net personal income growth.

Larger Transaction Sizes. The NavSTAR Client Acquisition System helps trusted advisors focus not just on the number of deals but also the size of the deal. Increasing transaction size can significantly affect gross income and net personal income growth.

More Profitable Client Acquisition. A culprit for lower gross profit client acquisition is discounting. Many trusted advisors have bought into the belief that discounting is the only way to close new business. The NavSTAR Client Acquisition System seeks to minimize discounting and raise gross profit margins.

Longer Client Retention. A proactive approach helps trusted advisors focus on retaining the "right" existing clients for a longer period of time. Extending client retention time frames can appreciably increase gross income and net personal income growth.

More Cost-Effective Lead Generation. One of the tragedies for trusted advisors is the number of wasted leads. Another tragedy is when leads are generated inefficiently and/or ineffectively. The NavSTAR Client Acquisition System will assist you in measuring your lead-generation cost-effectiveness.

Better ROI On Marketing. By eliminating lead waste, the natural result is an increased return on investment from marketing. The NavSTAR Client Acquisition System will assist you in measuring your marketing ROI.

Less Trusted Advisor Stress. Overall, the NavSTAR Client Acquisition System reduces stress on growth-minded trusted advisors. When trusted advisors have a client acquisition system they can count on, they can produce more predictable and sustainable client acquisition results.

The Voyage Begins With Personal Dreams

Before setting out on their voyage, a trusted advisor needs to determine their destination by specifying and documenting their personal dreams, the things they really want out of life for themselves and their loved ones.

The best way to do this would be by developing a bucket list and/or a vision chart of their ideal life if they had all the time and money in the world to live that life.

Once a trusted advisor's personal dreams have been documented and internalized, now is the time to delve into how one's *professional goals* are aligned to support one's dreams by mapping out goals and action plans designed to ensure life abundance. The following story illustrates one such trusted advisor journey.

The Margaret Reynolds Story

If you tear up at a Hallmark card or movie, Margaret Reynolds might be the reason why. Reynolds began her career at Hallmark Cards Inc., where she held executive roles of general manager and lead strategic officer. She was known for her natural inquisitiveness and innovative inclinations, never resting with the status quo.

She became a trusted advisor when she opened her independent consulting practice in Kansas City in 2001, and by 2008 had added a second office in Nashville.

What was the key to her business development success? The answer is knowing the numbers.

Tracking metrics for leading indicators can provide an early warning system that is invaluable to any business, giving it more time to react and increasing the probability of achieving breakthrough growth.

"Leading indicators are measures of progress on key variables that determine if the strategy is working," says Reynolds, author of the 2015 book that coauthor Henry DeVries helped her publish, *Reignite: How Everyday Companies Spark Next-Stage Growth.*[3]

NavSTAR Client Acquisition System Strategy #3

The "Book Is The Starting Line" strategy: A book is the number one marketing tool, and a speech is the number one marketing strategy for trusted advisors to attract high-paying clients. A book is the best business card/brochure a trusted advisor could ever produce. The right book can be an asset to every trusted advisor on the team.

Her book is part of her proactive system. The book helps her speak regularly before C-level executives.

In her book and her talks, Reynolds explains: "Sometimes, as organizations track leading indicators and anticipate being off at year-end, they will perform short-term heroics to supplement strategic results, such as holding a fire sale."

Trusted advisors in rough income seas are frequently tempted to do the same thing.

"While this may help in the short run, leading indicators suggest that implementation is not achieving the desired results and either the implementation effort is falling short or the strategy needs to be revisited," says Reynolds, who authored a second book, *Boost Your GrowthDNA*, in 2019, as part of her smooth selling strategy.[4] A trusted advisor who wants to be seen as a thought leader does not author just one book.

The NavSTAR Client Acquisition System: An Overnight Success Thirty Years In The Making

If you are about to embark on a proactive business development voyage, you need to know who the skipper is and their first mate. Okay, so here is the truth about the skipper, straight up.

Lead author Craig Lowder, creator of the NavSTAR Client Acquisition System, didn't go to Harvard, didn't go to Stanford, and you won't find a bunch of letters after his name. "I once went as far as having MBA on my business card, but you won't find it there anymore," he says.

"Mine was a blue-collar family just outside the rust belt, where I learned that it's not only what you know, but how you apply it," says Lowder. "I learned a couple of other important lessons back then that still serve me today."

One is that teamwork is a critical component of success anywhere—whether you are playing shortstop on a baseball field or navigating the challenges of the global economy. That's why as president of his own business development consulting firm, Craig only works with trusted advisors who are willing to listen, think, and contribute to their own personal development and their company's success. Success comes to a team, not individuals.

Coauthor Henry DeVries has similar philosophies. Inspired by his business partner Mark LeBlanc's teachings, Henry has a profile of his ideal fit client he wants to work with on business development and book publishing.

Craig's second lesson is nothing beats experience. "I've been mentored by some of the best in the business—people like Brad Sugars, Verne Harnish, Larry Wilson, Jeffrey Gitomer, Keith Cunningham, and Mark LeBlanc—but I've learned the best teacher is experience," says Craig.

And Craig has had his share. During his thirty-plus years as a business development manager and trusted advisor, he has worked with over sixty B2B and B2C companies and individual trusted advisors, increasing their gross income by 22 to 142 percent the following year.

But it has not all been smooth sailing. Through it all, Craig has seen the good and the bad and, frankly, learned more from the bad than the good. There have been storms that tested him as a trusted advisor. It is a real-world perspective that guides his work with trusted advisors today.

That is the same perspective that guides this book: the secret of trusted advisor client acquisition is to develop and execute a comprehensive, proactive strategic client acquisition plan. Nothing else will do. Most trusted advisors only strike at this goal with half measures. To strike with full force, a trusted advisor must navigate six stars to chart the following course:

NavSTAR Client Acquisition System Strategy #15
Collect Measurement-Based Testimonials

A Sample Email

The following is a testimonial used with the CEO's permission (but not his name). The numbers tell what can happen with a proactive strategic client acquisition plan.

Good morning Craig,

Here is a review for Jan-June 2015 and July-Dec 2015 for new business since we implemented the business development process in July 2015. See attached spreadsheet for monthly results. Highlights are huge! This is for new business.

Period	Average New Face-to-face Calls	Average # Of Quotes	Average Quoted $	Average # Of Orders	Average $ Order Won	Average Success Ratio
1st Six Months	11	15	$184,680	1	$9,138	7%
2nd Six Months	23	31	$290,115	7	$42,413	20%
Percentage Delta	+201%	+207%	+157%	+656%	+464%	+285%

It demonstrates the need to keep business development people out of office pursuing new accounts. The numbers tell the story.

Sincerely,

Meet The NavSTAR Client Acquisition System

Ancient mariners used stars to chart the journey. Today, trusted advisors need to navigate the complex buying journey of their clients.

Trusted advisors who yearn for proactive, predictable, and sustainable client acquisition results need to be guided by these six stars.

Trusted advisors who yearn for proactive, predictable, and sustainable client acquisition results need to be guided by these six stars:

Targeting Is Star One. The first proactive step is to know who you want.

Messaging Is Star Two. When you find your *who*, use a message that is right for them.

Biz Dev Process Mapping Is Star Three. Map your process and eliminate any wasteful steps.

Biz Dev Success Scorecard Is Star Four. What gets measured gets managed.

Lead Generation Is Star Five. Generating a prospective lead is like getting an at bat in baseball. You cannot get a hit if you don't have an at bat.

Feed The Funnel Is Star Six. Like the shampoo bottle says: lather, rinse, repeat. The funnel is your pipeline of qualified prospects who have a problem you can help solve and a budget to solve the problem.

Each star deserves a chapter of explanation, which will be handled in the next part of this book.

PART II

The NavSTAR Client Acquisition System

3

Targeting Is Star One

*He determines the number of the stars and
calls them each by name.*

Psalm 147:4

There is an old adage: if an arrow does not hit the target, it is never the fault of the target.

So, whose fault is it? The archer's, of course.

Effective targeting is where The NavSTAR Client Acquisition System begins. If you do a better job of targeting, your conversion rate will be higher. Depending on your ideal client profile, you'll have more opportunities, a higher probability of winning larger deals, and a steadier deal flow.

The whole idea behind this is based on who you are as a trusted advisor. If you can plug in the right input numbers, it will tell you how much activity you need to generate to make your numbers. You can do it in gross revenue, or you can do it in terms of net personal income.

But it will all come to nothing if you do not know who you are aiming at.

Identify Your Target Market

Before a trusted advisor can generate solid prospect leads, they must clearly define the target prospect. What problem do you solve, and for whom?

A target market with a problem is not enough. Trusted advisors must find target clients that can afford and have the willingness to pay for what you want to charge.

A target market with a problem is not enough. Trusted advisors must find target clients that can afford and have the willingness to pay for what you want to charge.

Finding a target market takes time, effort, and a dedication many would-be trusted advisors are unwilling to give.

While researching this book, one attorney was asked what kind of law he practiced, and he replied: "Rent law. Any law that pays the rent."

In researching a target market, here are ten filter questions to ponder in the following order:

1. **Are you interested in solving the problems this group has?** If their problems do not energize you, that should be a nonstarter.

2. **Have you worked with any already?** Targeting prospects you have never worked with is possible but not probable. Prospects want a successful track record.

3. **Can they afford you?** Money isn't everything, but it is certainly one important thing.

4. **Are they willing to pay more for better service?** There is no winning the low-price provider game. You cash bigger

checks by providing better service to those willing to pay for it.

5. **Do they already know they need a trusted advisor like you?** You are waging an uphill battle if you must educate the prospect that they need a trusted advisor like you. Everyone knows they need tax help (some call the Sixteenth Amendment to the US Constitution the Accountant Full Employment Act).

6. **Are they numerous?** If you want to catch fish, you go to a fishing hole where the fish are. The more of them there are, the better the fishing will be. That's just math.

7. **Do you have few real competitors?** If this is an attractive market, it will attract other trusted advisors. Even if you discover and create a new market, others will find it too. The trick is to offer a unique problem-solving process, which you document and name.

8. **Can you find them easily enough through lists and associations?** Demographics matter. You should be able to define with numbers your target market. Psychographics are well and good, but it's hard to find a list.

9. **Can you find a target-rich environment where they gather?** Again, to the fishing hole metaphor. If you prefer, what is their watering hole? What do they read, and what do they attend? You can Google that stuff (we know we used a noun as a verb).

10. **Will some make marquee clients, advocates, and references?** This might be a hush-hush group that never wants it known that you helped them. That will make it hard to demonstrate a successful track record in your testimonials.

Trusted advisors will need to do some old-fashioned homework but have no fear, new search techniques are here to help.

Name The Pain Like Lee

Interviewing prospects is part of a trusted advisor's pain research.

When trusted advisors find pain and challenges prospects are experiencing during a discovery conversation, they might fantasize the deal is as good as done. But the reality is different.

"When trusted advisors hear prospect challenges, they start licking their chops because they believe the door has opened to their solution," says author Lee Salz. "Unfortunately, many of them become disappointed when their deals never advance past the initial conversation."

According to Salz, trusted advisors are not asking enough questions to determine if the pain they have uncovered is an "inconvenience" or a "problem" for the prospect. Those two words are not synonymous.

During discovery, trusted advisors typically ask one type of question. However, in most cases, they should be asking two types.

"Initial scan questions are what I refer to as horizontal questions," says Salz. "These questions uncover 'the what.' They help you identify potential areas of pain or challenge that a prospect may be experiencing."

Trusted advisors typically neglect to ask what he calls vertical questions. These questions uncover "the why."

Vertical questions are intended to comprehensively analyze the pain/challenge the prospect is experiencing to determine the proper course of action.

For example, a trusted advisor might tell me they asked the prospect when they wanted a new system implemented. The prospect responded, "In August."

The trusted advisor wrote down "August" in his notes and moved on to the next surface-level question.

Asking: "When would you like to see a new system implemented?" is an example of a horizontal question. It tells you "the what" but not "the why." Horizontal questions do not provide you with the tools needed to advance the deal because of the unknown "why" behind it. That's what vertical questions provide.

"The mystery solver in me wants to know so much more than the date the prospect wants a new system implemented," says Salz. "In this case, capturing the desired installation date is merely a data point. By itself, it does not provide what you need to keep your deal energized and win it at the prices you want. You may think the deal is progressing, but it hasn't moved an inch."

More important, points out Salz, you lack the information to keep the deal moving forward, which becomes painfully apparent when expected award dates don't happen and deals evaporate.

Develop An Ideal Profile Of Your Perfect Fit Client

Here are samples from coauthors Craig Lowder and Henry DeVries.

Craig Lowder Ideal Client Top Fifteen Characteristics

1. Is an independent consultant or professional advisor
2. Works in North America
3. Is between the ages of twenty-five and sixty-five
4. Has a personal income of at least $100,000
5. Over the past several years, personal income has been stagnant, declining, or increasing gradually but not predictably

6. Wants to significantly grow their book of business and personal income by landing more high-paying clients

7. Are entering a new market or launching a new service that does not fit within their current business model

8. Is relationship oriented, not transaction focused

9. Recognizes that business development is not one of their core competencies

10. Is ready to make changes to the way they grow their book of business and realizes the need for professional assistance

11. Views personal development as an investment, not an expense

12. Is a believer in "systems" and is always seeking to do things better

13. Is a self-starter

14. Is a lifetime learner

15. Is enjoyable to work with

When you are talking to a prospective client for me, please refer them to my website or have them contact me directly via email or call.

Henry DeVries Ideal Client Top Ten Characteristics

1. Is a small to midsized ad or digital marketing agency owner

2. Wants to write and/or publish a book that they are proud of
3. Wants more credibility, impact, and influence
4. Currently has five to 200 employees
5. Is relationship minded, not transaction focused
6. Is between the ages of thirty-five and fifty-five
7. Has high integrity
8. Is enjoyable to work with
9. Works in North America
10. Their DiSC behavioral style: high D, I, or S preferred

When you are talking to a prospective ideal client for me, please recommend them to one of my monthly no-cost Q&As on Zoom or have them contact me directly via email or call.

Listen Better Like Chris Stiehl

Chris Stiehl, an independent research consultant who calls himself "The Listening Coach," has built a career on helping people listen.

"Your target prospects are talking, but are you really listening?" asks Stiehl, a human-factors engineer who has worked for the Cadillac division of General Motors, the US Coast Guard, and even the Nuclear Regulatory Commission.

"At Cadillac, we spent about $20,000 on a Voice of the Customer project that saved the company $3 million per year going forward," says Stiehl, who notes that a lack of listening is not just a North American problem. "We have conducted listening research in India, China, Brazil, Singapore, Kuala Lumpur, and Switzerland, as well as Canada and the United States."

During conversations with a prospect, the goal of a trusted advisor should be to monopolize the listening.

During conversations with a prospect, the goal of a trusted advisor should be to monopolize the listening. A good rule of thumb is to listen 80 percent of the time and talk 20 percent.

These are the three proven steps for success when it comes to listening carefully and responding appropriately:

1. **Identify the issue.** What is on their mind? Why did they reach out to you? What is their goal, what assets do they have in place, and what are their roadblocks? Ask questions to find out and listen carefully.

2. **Listen for the prospect's mindset.** This is not about good and bad people; this is about how they view the world at this point in time. Are they a thinker, a doer, a struggler, or an achiever? Again, ask questions and listen carefully.

3. **Respond in a way that meets what that person wants and needs.** To respond appropriately requires matching your language to the mindset of the prospect. Say the appropriate words that the prospect needs to hear.

NavSTAR Client Acquisition Strategy #13

This is the "Pain-Into-Gain Riddle" strategy. Your target prospects experience their unique frustrations and pains. As the old adage states, "People don't care what you know until they know that you care." Truly identifying your prospect's predicament tells them you understand and empathize with them.

The Pain-Into-Gain Listening Riddle

How will prospects hire you unless they trust you?
How, in turn, will they trust ideas they have not heard?
How, in turn, will they hear without someone to speak?
How, in turn, will you speak unless you have a solution?
How, in turn, will you have a solution unless you understand their pain?
How will you understand their pain unless you listen carefully?
How will you prove you listened unless you respond appropriately?

"A" Is For Awesome Target Client

There are several characteristics to consider for an awesome target prospect for a trusted advisor:

Demographics. Demographic data (the *who*) is used by trusted advisors to help them understand the characteristics of the people who buy their products and services. With demographics, you can see who your brand appeals to the most by age, location, gender, job title, income, time in business, industry, order size, and hundreds of other variables.

Geographics. Geographic data (the where) is used by trusted advisors to help them understand the characteristics of the people who buy their products and services. With geographic data, you can see where buying decisions are made and where products and services are to be delivered.

Psychographics. Psychographic data (the how) is the psychological study of buyers and their attitudes, interests, personalities, values, opinions, and lifestyles. In other words, how they go about making buying decisions. Buyers are typically looking to achieve stated "professional (or business) results" and, in many cases, unstated "personal wins," like making their jobs easier or not working as many hours.

What Are The Benefits Of Targeting?

You have two choices: spray-and-pray client acquisition or targeted client acquisition. With spray-and-pray, you spray your message everywhere and pray for the phone to ring.

To use a baseball metaphor, you are going to get more at bats with qualified prospects, and your batting average is going to go up too.

Targeted client acquisition is harder up front but makes your life so much easier in the end. Life is easier because you will have higher lead-to-client acquisition conversion rates. In other words, to use a baseball metaphor, you are going to get more at bats with qualified prospects, and your batting average is going to go up too.

Not only will you have a higher batting average, but it will also take you less time to land high-paying clients because it will shorten client acquisition cycles. These cycles refer to the series of events that typically take place for you to land a client.

When you know what client you want, finding them is easier. This means you will have more cost-effective lead generation. Generating a lead is not free. Each lead takes time and money. If you do not yet track your cost per lead, it is high time to begin.

Finally, you will be surprised how targeting helps build longer-lasting, value-based relationships. When you target, you will become better known within the target group. As the old adage goes, birds of a feather flock together. And they also move among the flock. Put another way, they like to bring their trusted relationships with them when they change organizations.

4

Messaging Is Star Two

Keep your eyes on the stars and your feet on the ground.

President Theodore Roosevelt

There's an old joke in marketing that if you do not have something distinguishing to advertise about your business, then you should advertise your business for sale.

Trusted advisors need to think about distinguishing, not differentiating.

Effective messaging is all about distinguishing yourself in your prospect's mind versus the competitive options they have in front of them. In other words, finding your "value wedge."

Steps To Find Your Value Wedge

The concept of a value wedge is best displayed as a Venn diagram. Three things are important to find what is called your value wedge. (This concept is taken from the book *Conversations That Win the Complex Sale* by Erik Peterson and Tim Riesterer).[5]

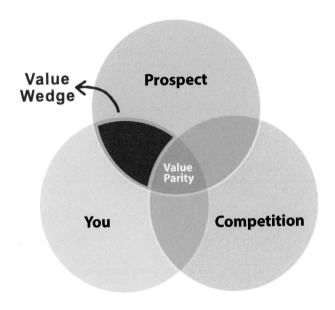

Circle number one: Prospect. What is really important to your prospective client? You have completed the critical first step if you understand what's most important in your prospect's world.

Circle number two: You. Overlay that with what you do exceptionally well. Identify the areas that are both important to your prospect and that you do exceptionally well. This overlap is essential, but it is not the whole picture.

Circle number three: Competition. Overlay that with what is important to your prospect, that you do exceptionally well, and that your competitors can't do—or, even if they claim to do it, they don't have any proof points to demonstrate their success. This third overlay is the value wedge.

Having taught this concept over a hundred times, I have heard a lot of folks say, well, we're not any different from the competition. *Not true*, there are always ways to distinguish yourself.

The place that you do not want to play is in an area called "value parity," which is the area where all three circles overlap. This is the area that is very important to your prospect, and you do it exceptionally well, but your competitors can claim exactly the same thing. Typically, value parity encompasses well over 80 percent of the area of the three circles, implying that an opportunity exists for you to create a value wedge; however, it may not be easy to identify without proper due diligence.

Remember, the prospect has options. You are not the only choice. So, in this Venn diagram, you are looking for your value wedge.

Typically, we help trusted advisors who think they are no different than their competitors come up with at least three to five significant differentiators. That's where your messaging needs to focus on areas your competition can't do, but you can do extremely well and have proof points. This is the value wedge.

Message Pyramid

It is the best practice to create a "value proposition" for your business so that your target audience views your products/services as both important to their success and unique.[6]

The message you create is your value proposition, which should include three points of distinction.

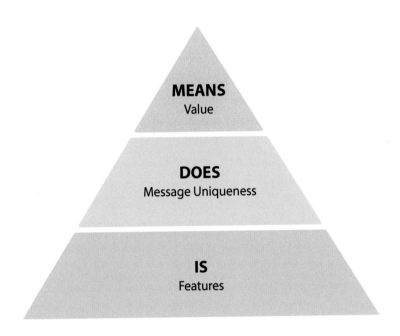

Differentiating With A Proprietary Process

Sometimes a line from a movie says it all.

Remember when every burger joint had a "secret sauce"? In the film *Fast Times at Ridgemont High*, teenage workers from two different fast-food restaurants reveal what goes into the secret sauce for their hamburgers. One says, "ketchup and mayonnaise," and the other says, "thousand island dressing."

Make sure that some real problem-solving ingredients have gone into your secret sauce—your proprietary process—and that the name actually reflects your unique approach.

So, what is your trusted advisor secret sauce?

When potential clients tell you their problems, they expect you to tell them how you can solve them. This is the moment of truth:

the time you explain how you solve problems like theirs. After you outline your path to a solution, you want them to think, "At last… a trusted advisor who understands my problem and really knows what they are doing."

To woo and win clients, trusted advisors could benefit from a distinct problem-solving methodology. This is your proprietary process, an approach unique to you or your firm. This must be included in a business advice book for a consultant or services business.

If you go to the Google search engine and type in "proprietary process," you will discover 20,000 entries. The proprietary process is gaining currency in the marketplace as a marketing technique. Nashville-based business consultant David C. Baker says one of the most common mistakes a trusted advisor can make is not having a defined, proprietary process. Baker highlights several reasons why a proprietary process is important.

"Process is differentiating, highlighting the uniqueness of your firm with a process that you own," says Baker. Other advantages he cites are that a process demonstrates your experience, makes your work less accidental, and will even allow you to charge more. "Clients are always willing to pay more for packages than individual hours within a fee structure."

A good proprietary process, however, is never a cut-and-dried industry standard lifted from a textbook. Instead, it codifies a firm's particular method of problem-solving, typically identifying and sequencing multiple steps that often occur in the same, defined order.

Furthermore, the completed process should have an intriguing name—one that you can trademark. What are some of these intriguing proprietary process names?

Here are a few to ponder:

- The NavSTAR Client Acquisition System
- The I-Innovation Process
- The SupporTrak RACE System
- The NetRaker Methodology
- The Systematic Determination Process
- The Persuasion Iteration Process

Don't worry if you don't understand what these processes do just by hearing the names; that's the point. A name that is unique enough actually to qualify to be trademarked will also create the opportunity to explain the process to potential clients. Don't go overboard, however, and create a name that is all marketing hype with no real service substance.

Your messaging is how you distinguish yourself from other trusted advisors seeking to attract the same type of client.

If you can't communicate a brand, you are offering yourself as a generic commodity, which is no way to attract high-paying clients.

If you can't communicate a brand, you are offering yourself as a generic commodity, which is no way to attract high-paying clients.

Every trusted advisor is different, and all can benefit from a mix of the ten ways to communicate the message, which are, in alphabetical order:

Advertising. Controlled media channels that you pay to get your message out in collateral, print ads, radio ads, internet ads, and TV ads. This can include advertising in directories published by associations representing your target audience.

Direct Mail. Sending email and snail mail to a targeted list of prospects with an offer. The best is direct mail invitations to events you host.

Networking. Attending business events with the intent of meeting others and offering to be of service to them. You should network at events that are target-rich environments. You need a defining statement that makes clear who you serve and the outcomes they obtain.

Proprietary Process. This is a trademarked way of solving client problems. Give the process a name and take the steps to trademark the process, which communicates this is a key part of your brand.

Proprietary Research. Conduct periodic research about your target audience's frustrations, concerns, and wants. Publish the results.

Publicity. Obtaining exposure through articles and interviews in newspapers, websites, blogs, books, trade journals, magazines, social media, radio, and television. Have prepared sound bites ready to deliver to communicate the brand.

Showcases. These include speaking engagements, self-hosted workshops, webinars, Zoom seminars, online videos, and live webcasts. Be generous in providing information on how prospects can solve their problems in general; they are more apt to hire you for the specifics.

Social Media And Websites. Social media, like LinkedIn and YouTube, should supplement your brand marketing, not be your marketing. A website should build credibility by demonstrating your expertise.

Telemarketing. Making phone calls to prospects. As one author buddy of mine says, "Pick up the dang phone." Coauthor Henry calls the registered attendees of his workshops the day before the workshop just to tell them he is looking forward to meeting them.

Trade Shows. Purchasing space to set up a booth or table at sponsored product and service expos. If this works in your world, it is an excellent way for prospects to experience real humans embodying the brand.

NavSTAR Client Acquisition System Strategy #14

The "Offer Advice In General" strategy. Research shows trusted advisors can fill a pipeline with qualified clients in as little as thirty days by offering prospects advice on overcoming pressing problems if they have the right marketing DNA.

However, before you can begin attracting clients with books and speeches, you need to create a biz dev genetic code that is attractive to clients. All your marketing messages, from networking discussions to speeches, will contain the elements of this marketing DNA that positions you as a thought leader.

Create Your Own Biz Dev Genetic Code

Here are ten steps that trusted advisors can use to improve their marketing appeal:

Step One. Name your business without your name. Create a business name or a website name that gives potential clients a hint at the results you can produce for them. The worst possible business name or website name is your name.

Step Two. Boil it down. Write a headline for your website and marketing materials that describes your audience and the results you produce for them. Do this in no more than ten words.

Step Three. Name your client's pain. What are your client's worries, frustrations, and concerns that you help solve? This is also called the FUD factor: fear, uncertainty, and doubt.

Step Four. How to fix it. Describe your solution or methodology for solving these pains. What process do you follow to produce results? Offering a proprietary problem-solving process that you name and trademark is best. This answers the all-important question in their minds: "Why should I do business with you instead of one of your competitors?"

Step Five. The myths. State the common misperceptions that hold many back from getting results. Why doesn't every trusted advisor do what you do?

Step Six. Step by step. Tell your clients what they need to do in general to solve their problems.

Step Seven. The extras. List other benefits they get from following your methods and working with you as a trusted advisor.

Step Eight. Track record. Elaborate on your track record of providing measurable results for clients. Be as specific as possible. Use numbers, percentages, and time factors as proof points.

Step Nine. Give it away. Create a website with free-tip articles on how to solve these pains. Each article should be between 300 and 600 words. Each tip can be numbered so it can be read easily.

Step Ten. Make an offer they can't refuse. Offer prospects a free special report on your website. You are offering to trade them valuable information for their email address. Tell them they will also receive a tips e-newsletter from you. Assure them you will maintain their privacy, and they can easily opt out of your list anytime.

Embed Messages Into Stories

Do you want more high-paying clients? It pays to spin a good yarn.

Stories about clients you have helped solve a problem can establish your credibility in under two minutes.

Start by focusing on the worst part of the story.

"It's a surprise of sorts," says award-winning author Dave Lieber. "The best part of any story is the worst part. Don't skip through it."

Lieber, a certified professional speaker, is an expert at teaching storytelling in business. He shows individuals, businesses, and industries how to use stories to meet their goals.

"The low point of a good business story is the most important part. So why do you keep rushing through it?" asks Lieber.

Discoveries in neurosciences prove people make decisions based on emotion, not logic. These are emotional times, and if you want to attract more high-paying clients, you need to become a better business storyteller who reaches the emotional part of the brain.

"Every good story has a beginning, middle, and end," says Lieber. "Every good story has a hero and a villain. And most good stories have a happy ending that symbolizes accomplishment and offers an important lesson."

Lieber has honed his craft as the national-award-winning "Watchdog" columnist for the *Dallas Morning News*. (His fish-out-of-water stories about moving from the East Coast to Texas are solid gold.) We met when he spoke at a conference I hosted for new authors.

"But I've noticed that most business storytellers ignore the most important part of the story," says Lieber. "They fail to emphasize the low point, the worst part of the story for the hero. The problem that needs to be solved."

The author of nine books, Lieber is also a playwright with two plays staged in the Dallas-Fort Worth area and elsewhere in Texas.

If the story shows it was easy for the hero, that is boring. Some business storytellers like to skip the middle struggle part of the story.

"Here's why that's a big mistake: we learn more from our failures and struggles than we do from our successes," says Lieber. "When the hero decides to take a giant step out of the low point and beat back the villain, we learn a tremendous amount of helpful information."

According to Lieber, we lose learning opportunities when the low point is slighted and quickly passed over to get to the climactic ending.

"That's why as a writer, keynote speaker, and trainer, I teach clients to dwell in the low point," says Lieber. "Live there in the story long enough for the audience to feel the discomfort. Put the audience in the middle of the story. Make them feel some of the confusion, the difficulties, and the challenge of the low point."

When this is done properly, the journey out of the low point to the climax is more emotional and memorable.

"By the ending, lessons are learned and not forgotten," says Lieber.

Messaging Is Personal Branding

"When it comes to messaging and branding, don't overthink it."[7]

That is the advice to trusted advisors from branding expert Yali Saar.

Saar is the CEO and cofounder of Tailor Brands, a venture-backed startup company using artificial intelligence (AI) to teach computers to design logos, write copy, and even plan content strategy.

"How long should you spend working on your brand?" asks Saar. "A month? A quarter? I'm happy to tell you that both of these time frames are too long."

Branding today is about speed, says Saar. Prior to Tailor Brands, Saar was a journalist, political spokesperson, and cofounder of Raising the Bar, a worldwide education initiative with hundreds of members in New York, San Francisco, Sydney, and Hong Kong.

Branding is about creating a positive image in the consumers' minds.

Branding is about creating a positive image in the consumers' minds. Here are three branding tips from Saar to speed up the process:

It's not about you; it's about them. The first question every person asks during the branding process is, "Does this represent me and my mission?" While aligning your brand with your vision is important, putting it at the center of your brand-building process will prevent you from looking at the most important thing: your customers. Saar says, "Your vision was created to solve a problem or answer a need, so instead of asking whether or not your brand represents you first, ask yourself whether or not it represents your clients and the reason they need your service."

Make sure even a child can understand it. One of the most repeated questions Saar hears is, "How can I make my brand unique?" The simple answer is you shouldn't. What's the best test to ensure your brand is memorable? Show it to a nine-year-old and ask them to repeat it. Saar says, "Did you pass the test? Great!" You didn't? Then simplify. Don't try to make their brains work too hard. Brains are lazy and won't do it (actually, brains conserve energy).

Personal brands are about continuity. "We live in a multiplatform world," says Saar. People will bump into your brand in the street, visit your site, and search for it on Google. As businesses become easier to set up, customers do their due diligence to understand exactly what your brand is all about. Nothing is more distrustful than a personal brand that shows different faces depending on its platform.

"While we would all like to be pro golfers who manage to hit a hole-in-one, brand building is an iterative process," says Saar. "You need to try things out and see how they resonate with your clients."

So instead of trying to build the message on the first go, test messaging as soon as possible and be sure to collect feedback so you'll know how to adjust as fast as possible.

5

⚜

Biz Dev Process Mapping
Is Star Three

There is no easy way from the earth to the stars.

Roman philosopher Seneca

Too many trusted advisors are just winging it. They do not have a map for their business development processes.

Prospects have a road map for hiring a trusted advisor like you. Every prospect has a buyer's journey. Do you know what the road map they are following looks like?

Every prospect has a buyer's journey. Do you know what the road map they are following looks like?

Business development process mapping is the best practice of identifying and documenting the most direct path from a prospect becoming a client. Effective business development processes mirror the prospective client's buying journey.

Typically, at least three business development processes need to be mapped. These processes are:

New Client Acquisition. Most trusted advisors start here and stop here. Who makes the decision, and how do they make it? Who else gets involved? How many alternatives will the prospect examine? You can trust that the prospect always has options.

Existing Client Upselling Or Cross-Selling. An existing client is an asset. One way to increase billings is to offer clients complementary services. This can be a sliver of gold in your database. You should surface new opportunities for the client. They would rather buy from someone they already trust, like you, than vet a new relationship.

Past Client Reorder. There is an old joke that there are no former clients, just recovering clients. Think of all those clients you did business with in the past. History can be a great predictor of the future. Those who worked with you before are highly likely to work with you again if you approach them in the right way. There is an anecdote about a stranger who contacted a law firm and said, "Okay, we need you, let's get started." It took the law firm some research to discover this was a client from ten years previous who was on the newsletter list. "We've always considered you to be our law firm. We just did not need your help again until now," said the client.

Understanding The Buyer's Journey

Are you practicing good business development or bad business development?

Some comprehensive research at LinkedIn examined 10,000 different perspectives from buyers around the world.

"Some companies are absolutely in distress mode," says Alyssa Merwin of LinkedIn. "There are other companies that are frozen, and they're trying to figure out how do we adjust and adapt our business to this new environment and figure out a way forward. And there are other companies certainly that are thriving in this environment and are well positioned to take advantage of the opportunities ahead of them."

Merwin, vice president of sales solutions in North America at LinkedIn, oversees a team of 350 sales professionals. Merwin has nearly twenty years of experience connecting buyers and sellers and is dedicated to helping trusted advisors modernize their methods and mindsets.

Of course, she noted that due to the pandemic, buyer's journeys today look vastly different than before 2020.

"There really is starting to be a bifurcation between good behavior and bad behavior," says Merwin.

We want to encourage trusted advisors to think about that: which of those camps are you in? Are you a good advisor or a bad advisor? Are you being naughty or nice? The good and nice thing to do is to put buyers first.

Research at LinkedIn indicates four key ways trusted advisors can put the buyer first:

Learn, then deliver helpful content. You do not necessarily have to write original content, but trusted advisors must build their brands by sharing content. "That's going to help bring credibility and add value to the demographic they want to engage," says Merwin. She notes that each buyer's situation is unique, and there are nuances to the challenges they face. Get curious. Ask questions to understand their industry, business, role, what they're solving for, what success looks like for them, their timing, their dependencies, and their process. Offer help, not hype.

Share readily. Trusted advisors need to come better equipped to the conversations with a perspective to share an insight. Merwin says: "It can't be all about making the deal." She urges trusted advisors to share trends, insights, and learnings specific to the buyer's industry that show you're an expert and build trust.

Solve before selling. In their research, one of the starkest differences that LinkedIn found was the difference between what buyers want and what trusted advisors are prioritizing. "An example of this is that from a buyer's perspective, the number one skill they value in building trust in a relationship is active listening. That is the number one requested skill." Guess where that ended up on the list of the people meeting with them? "It is laughable, number seven," says Merwin.

Earn trust. "We're seeing 40 percent more people making warm introductions, which we would advocate as a good selling behavior," says Merwin. Build a trusted relationship by acting consistently in the buyer's interest during each step of their journey. Invest in the long term, even if it means sacrifices in the short term. Merwin advises becoming a trusted advisor by listening to the buyer's specific challenges, crafting solutions that help them achieve their goals, and surfacing new opportunities that show them what is possible.

Each buyer's challenges may look different, but one thing is consistent: buyers need to feel confident that you understand their challenges and goals. In the end, you are not necessarily selling a product or service, you are selling a trusted relationship, and the person at the center of that relationship is the buyer.

Virtual Business Development And Process Mapping

Sure, the pandemic forced many trusted advisors to embrace that newfangled virtual world while longing for the days of in-person business development. But is virtual business development really new for trusted advisors?

Many companies would have you believe virtual business development is new and constitutes a huge paradigm shift for them. But does it? Virtual business development has been around for over a hundred years; think catalogs, newspapers, direct mail offers, late-night TV infomercials, telemarketers, and e-commerce.

What *is* different is how traditional trusted advisors started interacting with their buyers due to the pandemic and the need for social distancing.

Virtual selling is here to stay. Expect it to grow exponentially over the coming years and decades. Both buyers and sellers realize the unexpected benefits of virtual selling and buying. According to Lowder, to become an effective virtual seller, sellers must consider six key building blocks:

Buyer's Journey. Everything starts with this. Changes in the buyer decision process will necessitate that trusted advisors adjust their business development processes to accommodate the new buyer journey. Think more of the journey on Zoom and the phone.

Messaging. New digital sales marketing communication tools need to be created to gain potential buyers' attention, fully engage with them, and develop buyer relationships. Short and highly visual messages, including video, will be a must. Watching videos is now part of the journey.

Meeting Cadence. Virtual meetings, in terms of their *length* (less than forty-five minutes), *frequency* (more often), and *pace* (fast), must be thoroughly grasped by trusted advisors to connect with buyers.

Biz Dev KPIs/Scorecards. Business development key performance indicators, activities, and results must be attuned to a virtual environment.

Technology. Virtual business development relies on a working knowledge of audio, visual, and lighting communications systems and tools to engage and build a relationship with buyers.

People. The people and communication skills they must master are essential to effective virtual business development and require thorough scrutiny.

Here is why virtual business development is here to stay. Buyers benefit from the ease of scheduling virtual meetings, shorter duration meetings, and a greater number of buying influences participating in virtual meetings. That results in both productivity gains and better decisions. Trusted advisors are realizing similar benefits in productivity gains, reduced business development costs, and, in many cases, shorter sales cycles.

Trusted Advisors Must Up Their Game On Zoom

Patrick McGowan has some hard news for trusted advisors: people are judging you on Zoom. Because much of the buyer's journey is now virtual, there are serious ramifications for trusted advisors.

"Amateur hour is over," says McGowan, founder of Punch'n, a video presence company. "The days of looking like a *Dateline* interview of someone from the Witness Protection Program must be behind us."

Having to live your work life on Zoom is hard. The most popular quote of the pandemic will be, "You are on mute." And worse, making comments when you don't realize you are not muted. And, as actor Seth Rogen tweeted, "I call my Zoom meeting look 'laced up from the waist up.'"

Another favorite tweet from Snarky Mommy is: "There's awkward, and then there's 'the Zoom meeting is over, and you and one other person can't figure out how to leave the meeting' awkward."

"We need to approach our video meetings with the same level of care and intentionality as we do our in-person meetings," says McGowan, who works with people who want to level up their video presence. "How we show up defines us and defines our personal brand."

McGowan reminds us of the adage that a picture is worth a thousand words. "But a video is worth 10,000 words. At thirty frames per second, the camera doesn't lie."

Zoom fatigue can be remedied with a strong purpose. "When we are intentional about bringing our best self to our video events, our authentic self and our value get communicated, and we make a positive impression."

Here are four tips from McGowan on how to improve your personal brand through Zoom:

Show up five minutes early. "Every pilot goes through a flight check to make sure *all systems are go*. We should do the same thing if we want to make a positive impression. I often launch a 'New Appointment' on Zoom to check that I have the right camera, microphone, and speaker selected. I'll exit that meeting on Zoom and then log in to the scheduled appointment. Additionally, we can all schedule meetings for forty-five minutes rather than sixty minutes. Different times get different rules."

Frame yourself. "We want to use the Rule of Thirds to position ourselves a little off-center. Shifting to the left or right of center and having your eyes at about a third of the way down from the top positions you in a photographically ideal position. This shows you are intentional about how you appear on camera and subtly communicates that you are someone to watch. To achieve this, folks often stack a small pile of books (cookbooks work really well) and place the camera at about eyebrow-level and then angle it slightly downward about five to ten degrees. I recommend to start with a webcam rather than a laptop camera and to put it on a small, desktop tripod, which allows you to tilt the camera."

Comfort = Confidence. "When I first began to use Zoom on a regular basis, I used either my laptop camera or a webcam. I didn't feel like I could sit naturally or comfortably for either. Through this, I discovered how much I contorted my body, shoulders, and neck to fit into the view of the camera. This is one reason why I recommend starting with a webcam rather than a laptop camera and to put it on a small desktop tripod with the ability to tilt the camera. Framing yourself sitting comfortably gives your team, audience, and viewers a sense of calm. It also begins to define your video presence."

Let them see your eyes. "While we are biologically drawn to look at people's faces when we can, on video calls it's vital we let our viewers see our eyes. This means we have to become comfortable looking at the camera instead of our monitor. This takes practice and time to develop our own personal style of presenting over video. At thirty frames per second, we have to realize the camera doesn't lie. When people can see our eyes, we are more approachable and watchable."

A bonus tip from McGowan is to focus on viewers. He says this is pretty easy: shut off Self View, then stop thinking about what you look or sound like on video.

"We want to shift our focus to why we are in this meeting or virtual event," says McGowan. "For most of us, we have something to give that is of value to another human being. We want to ultimately connect with someone. It's near impossible to focus on other people when we're looking at ourselves in the mirror."

Everything needs to start with understanding your target audience and the buying journey they will take. Put your buyer's hat on for a minute. If you were deciding to hire a trusted advisor like you, what steps would you go through to make the best decision?

Develop a checklist that you think they will follow. Test this by asking prospects how they make decisions like this.

That way, the client prospect believes that they're in control, but the reality is you are because you're always just one step ahead of them. Since you know what information they need, you provide it in advance.

If A Beauty Contest Or Bakeoff Is Part Of The Journey

If you want to win high-paying clients, you need to consider a specific part of the buyer's journey. Today's buyer buys differently than in the past when trusted advisors would help them with information and options. That has all changed because there has been a shift in the marketplace.

"Thanks to self-guided online research and digital marketing, up to 80 percent of the buyer's journey is now complete before you as a trusted advisor even enters the picture," according to author Bryan Gray of the book *The Priority Sale.*[8]

This has created what Gray terms "the last mile dilemma." The hardest part of any race is the last mile. The presentation showdown is the last mile.

But know this; the race may not be on a level track. The last mile, also known as the pitch or bakeoff or beauty contest, may be rigged against you.

Every trusted advisor "loathes the so-called competitive bakeoff," writes author Tim Riesterer[9]. "That's when customers round up all the leading providers in a given product or service category and make them beat each other. There are few real winners in the competitive bakeoff."

Do you ever suspect that prospects are using the bakeoff and beauty contest request for proposals (RFPs) just for information gathering? If you feel this way, you are not alone. Here is an example from the investment banking world.

"Sometimes the bank that wins the bakeoff was chosen in advance," according to author Matt Walker. "For example, Morgan Stanley may have already been preemptively chosen by the seller to market the assets, but they send out RFPs anyway for information gathering as these RFP responses can be robust."

Not all races are rigged. Sometimes you have a chance to win. Albeit typically a one-in-three chance to win (to quote NASCAR legend, Dale Earnhardt, "Second place is just the first loser.")

"The internet hasn't been kind to the trusted advisor," says Gray, a trusted advisor and founder of Revenue Path Group.

Before the internet, prospects needed a trusted advisor to obtain information. That meant that as soon as a prospect entered the marketplace, they were in touch with viable options.

"Today, that's not the case," says Gray. "Prospects delegate a lot of research to a lower-level employee, who brings options to the table. By the time they make contact, they have decided their own solution, pigeonholed you in with some competitors, and want you to compete on price."

The importance of the internet and social media is not news. But like many other aspects of marketing, the pandemic has dramatically accelerated this shift. This has a huge impact on the business development process.

"Looking back at the pandemic of 2020, this is the fastest the business world has ever changed," says Gray, who I met when I helped him edit his first sales and marketing strategy book. "But looking forward, this time will seem slow compared to future acceleration."

To apply an old movie line to the shift, "You ain't seen nothing yet."

Motorsports fans are familiar with the last mile dilemma. Ask Indy car driver J.R. Hildebrand. After leading the race, he lost the 2011 Indianapolis 500 in the final turn. Or driver Takuma Sato, who lost the 2012 Indy 500 on the final lap. And don't forget Will Power, who lost the 2015 Indy 500 in the last mile.

But here is the problem for trusted advisors: it is a winner-take-all game. The winning trusted advisor wins it all. Every other trusted advisor ties for second place and receives zero, zilch, nothing. Sometimes the buying company that brings in the competing trusted advisors decides not to hire anybody at this time, and then nobody wins. When the buying company opts to delay taking action, every trusted advisor ties in second place. And there is no money in second place.

"When you consider your leads-to-win ratio, studies have shown your biggest enemy today isn't your direct competitor," says Gray. "Yes, they do get their fair share of wins. But 60 percent of all opportunities are lost because the prospect decides to do nothing or stay with the incumbent."

6

Biz Dev Success Scorecard
Is Star Four

Moonlight drowns out all but the brightest stars.

J. R. R. Tolkien, in *The Lord of the Rings*

You can't know the actual score without a scorecard. A business development success scorecard is how to track the metrics along the way to attracting a high-paying client.

Trusted advisors should adopt the best practice of using a scorecard to identify and document the key activities and results that will lead to achieving business development success.

The steps along the way are also known as key performance indicators or KPIs. Also known as key success indicators are the five to eight essential activities and results metrics that a trusted advisor should track.

Ten Great Metrics You Won't See On *Mad Men* Reruns

Mad Men is the American period drama television series about Madison Avenue advertising in the 1960s created by Matthew

Weiner. The series ran on the cable network AMC from 2007 to 2015, but its fictional time frame runs from 1960 to 1970.

Mad Men is a term coined in the 1950s to describe Madison Avenue advertising executives, brought to life in the popular TV show.

In the show Don Draper and the creative team sit around, staring into space, trying to come up with a big idea to pitch to a client. Once they convince the client that their idea is brilliant, it seems Don's job is done.

"With modern marketing, instead of taking a nap or going to a movie waiting for inspiration to strike, we look at data," says Michelle Stansbury, the founder of Little Penguin PR, a boutique public relations company in San Diego. "We have insights into customer trends, buying patterns, sales cycles, and conversion goals. While creativity is still essential, marketing pros should direct their creativity with a strategic and results-oriented approach."

The first step is that you will need to determine which metrics you're going to test before executing any specific strategy. What will you consider a success? Next, track metrics not just to prove that your campaign is successful, but to honestly learn from the most effective strategies.

Here are examples of ten metrics to track weekly or monthly, broken up into results and activities. Note that activities should be tracked and evaluated weekly, while results should be tracked weekly and evaluated monthly.

Activities That You Control

- Seed-planting emails, phone calls, and LinkedIn messages sent to prospects and referral sources.
- The gross number of prospects who are sent emails, like an opt-in tips newsletter.

- Meaningful conversations with prospects, which are leads generated by various tactics such as speaking, writing, and networking.

- Blogs or articles published on your website, your LinkedIn page, or on another internet site; YouTube videos posted; or podcast episodes produced.

- Showcase speeches made to target-rich audiences, either in person or virtually, or as a guest on a podcast.

- Attendance at networking events attended by a target-rich audience.

Results That You Influence By Your Activities

- Number and dollar value of new project proposals delivered.

- The number of proposals converted (your batting average) and average initial revenue generated per client.

- The number of new clients.

- The size of the prospect database consists of opt-in email addresses you obtain from prospects through networking, speaking, and websites; social media contacts such as LinkedIn first connections you make; and referral advocates in Microsoft Outlook or similar programs.

Business Development Is Like A Science Experiment

Think of lead generation and conversion like a series of science experiments. You have a theory, you test that theory with a hypothesis, and your lead generation and conversion efforts are the experiments that give you results. Track the results on your scorecard to make better decisions.

More is not better when it comes to metrics. When trusted advisors track too many metrics, they tend to fizzle and fade. So typically, there should be three to five activities and maybe two to three results on your scorecard.

Much depends on what you choose to focus on.

What are good target metric results and activities? Every trusted advisor is different.

Focus on the key indicators for you: the activities and the results that matter. For you, it might be different than the above list. For instance, some trusted advisors track revenue billed and the percentage of revenue collected. Others track the number of RFPs they respond to every week.

If you play the RFP game and want them on your scorecard, there are some serious issues for trusted advisors to consider.

If you play the RFP game and want them on your scorecard, there are some serious issues for trusted advisors to consider.

The True Cost Of Losing An RFP

Are you an RFP winner or loser?

According to Investopedia, an RFP is a business document that announces and provides details about a project and solicits bids from contractors who will help complete the project.

In many cases, governments only use requests for proposals to obtain contractors. The RFP process requires the issuing entity to review the bids to examine their feasibility, the health of the bidding company, and the bidder's ability to do what is proposed.

Lisa Rehurek is a trusted advisor disrupting the tired RFP game, bringing her down-to-earth, "get it done" personality and fresh approach to winning more business.[10]

After a successful twenty-five-year career in corporate leadership positions, Rehurek went out on her own to share her expertise and experience to improve RFP results for businesses of all sizes. She and her team at the RFP Success Company have trained hundreds of business development staff and helped organizations win over $50 million in new business.

We asked Rehurek—an eight-time author, national speaker/trainer, podcast host, and business builder—to offer advice on the actual cost of being a loser:

Money. "The most immediate effect of a lost RFP is the absence of new revenue. Companies depend heavily on their RFP/capture teams to secure opportunity wins on a consistent basis. New contracts equal new revenue, that's obvious. However, when a company loses an RFP opportunity, the ripple effect is felt throughout the company. When we win an RFP, we not only win the business now, but we have a much higher potential of winning the business into the future."

Lifetime Customer Value. "There is exponential future revenue potential in the customer that you win today. New contracts don't just equal new revenue in the now—they also create future revenue potential. Conversely, in addition to the potential contract amount that was up for bid, a failed RFP means the company has also lost the potential to repeatedly close with the new client/customer, or, at the very least, delayed the ability."

Hard Expenses. "Expenses spent completing a failed RFP can be a hard-hitting dose of reality. In addition to these hard expenses, companies incur a direct hit in terms of employee salary spend. What's interesting is that most companies never calculate this, therefore, this number is never known."

Industry Credibility. "Whether we like it or not, reputation matters. And a reputation precedes every RFP. In a recent article, RFPIO asserted peer recommendations influence about 90 percent of buying decisions. Successful companies become known in the marketplace. A buzz is created, and their name comes up in more conversations."

Internal Confidence. "RFP losses will eventually shake team confidence. When RFP and capture teams begin a downward spiral of consistent losses, team members begin to question the organization's market position, their colleagues' expertise, as well as their own. As team confidence wanes, team members begin experiencing task avoidance, indecision, and intrateam hostility while reporting increased levels of workplace stress. Is this the team you want in charge of creating a winning proposal? Knowing what each employee is motivated by is your job as leader. Among those factors are learning opportunities, recognition, harmony, competitiveness, serving the greater good, and structure. When they are rewarded for what they are motivated by, they will be deeply engaged."

Employee Retention. "Great team members stay with great teams. And great team members leave losing teams. High-performing, highly engaged team members are created through great leadership, achievements (which creates confidence), and commitment to purpose. Even the best all-star response teams begin to slowly fall apart after consecutive losses. Great team members want to work with *other* great team members. And they want to work for a winning organization. High performers know reputation matters, and staying at a company that continues to lose doesn't aid their professional goals."

The bottom line is, if you are going to play the RFP game, you better play it to win.

Use A Feedback Loop For Better SEO Results

Is search engine optimization, commonly known as SEO, an essential metric for you?

SEO optimization can be a tricky strategy that eludes even the best trusted advisors. But it has the potential to create huge results if done properly. And most of the time, it is not done correctly.

That's the view of Eli Schwartz, author of one of the top-selling books on SEO, who brings more than a decade of experience with big tech companies to the table.

"Too often, SEO efforts begin with just a group of keywords, developed by the marketing team or founders, based on their own knowledge of the product," says Schwartz, author of the contrarian book *Product-Led SEO.*[11] "Keyword-based SEO is limited and inadequate, and there is a better way."

Typically in SEO, keywords become the stems of keyword research. They are input into a keyword research tool, and related words are output.

"The new, longer list becomes the seed for content ideas that will be written and posted on the website. The problem?" asks Schwartz. "The keyword list becomes a checklist and content roadmap, which doesn't change much over time."

According to Schwartz, whatever the actual performance or real-time metrics, content keeps getting cranked out using the words from the original keyword checklist.

"In this paradigm of SEO, there's no room for a user's feedback loop," says Schwartz.

He advises that rather than develop a straight dictionary product like any other online translation library that merely targets one-to-one word definitions (Google included) and tries to jam as many keywords as possible onto the page; there is a better way. Build pages that are focused on user experience first.

Schwartz has helped clients like Shutterstock, WordPress, Blue Nile, Quora, and Zendesk execute highly successful global SEO strategies. As head of SurveyMonkey's SEO team, he oversaw the company's global operations, helped launch the first Asia-Pacific office, and grew the company's organic search as a key driver of global revenue.

Unfortunately, most of our modern-day SEO efforts ignore user feedback.

"Instead of focusing on the quality of the search experience for the user, we often focus on keywords and ignore the user's preferences almost entirely," says Schwartz.

7

Lead Generation Is Star Five

The sight of stars makes me dream.

Vincent Van Gogh

Dena Lefkowitz, a lawyer turned business coach, believes a preschool rhyme is worth remembering if you want to attract more high-paying clients.

"If you are a professional service provider, you've probably been exhorted to 'eat what you kill.' rather than relying on others to generate your work," says Lefkowitz. "The current emphasis on professionals selling reminds me of the beginning of *This Little Piggy* by Mother Goose: 'This little piggy went to market.' If your business depends on attracting clients, you must go to market."

What does "going to market" mean for today's trusted advisors?

"At the end of the day, you may want to go home," Lefkowitz rejoined. "You put in your hours, and the lure of the hearth beckons; however, work isn't done unless you've done something to get more clients. When you go home, there's a 100 percent chance you will not meet anyone who can give or send you business."

Lefkowitz has a national practice helping attorneys and executives increase career satisfaction by developing marketing strategies, boosting self-confidence, and learning essential skills for leading others. Lefkowitz graduated from Temple University School of Law and the College of Executive Coaching and regularly contributes to the *Legal Intelligencer*. She is certified by the International Coaching Federation.

What can a busy trusted advisor do to incorporate more networking and marketing into their current workday?

Lefkowitz has two suggestions: "First, adopt the mindset that getting work is as important as doing work, and you've got to find the time. Priorities may need adjusting. Second, make your extracurricular activities a blend of personally intriguing and professionally rewarding."

I asked for some specific extracurricular activities, and Lefkowitz was ready with a list:

Use Passion. "Pick something you're interested in so there will be a good chance of follow-through. An area of passion helps you stay engaged."

Make It A Target-Rich Environment. "Make sure there is a likelihood that your ideal clients or referral sources (someone who serves your ideal client in a different capacity) are involved with that organization or activity."

Vet The Group First. "Once you've targeted an activity or organization, vet it to make sure your valuable networking time is spent wisely."

Check The Schedule. "Look ahead and pick events. Register and put them on your calendar. Connect in advance with others who are attending or identify who you want to meet. Create these anchors that make it harder to blow networking off."

Ask And Listen. "Think ahead about how to present yourself. Who are you? What problem do you solve? Whom do you serve? These are good ingredients of an initial introduction. Have some icebreaker questions to ask, and listen carefully to what you hear. That's the gold you'll mine later."

Lefkowitz emphasizes the importance of making going to market a professionally satisfying activity; otherwise, you'll dread and avoid it. "You must go to market," she stresses, "so why not make it more fun by finding things you really care about and doing them with people you like, who you can help, and vice versa? You can make time for that, even when you're busy."

The James Ware Story

"Most meetings are a waste of time." That is the core lead-generation message that is building the trusted advisor practice of James Ware, a former Harvard Business School professor.

"We need to bring business meetings into the digital age in the same way that we have reinvented business planning and written communication," says Ware, author of the 2016 book *Making Meetings Matter: How Smart Leaders Orchestrate Powerful Conversations in the Digital Age.*[12]

Trusted advisor Ware has invested his entire career in understanding what organizations must do to thrive in a rapidly changing world. His business wisdom comes from deep academic knowledge and more than thirty years of hands-on experience as a senior executive and a change leader who drives corporate innovation.

Ware, who lives in Walnut Creek, California, says leaders should think of a meeting as an improv performance; the most important mindset you can establish is to have a basic plan but then to be in the moment, reacting both instinctively and creatively to events as they evolve in real time.

A great lead-generation strategy for Ware is speaking, but there are many effective new contact strategies. There are seven basic strategies for generating leads. Every trusted advisor is different, and all can benefit from a mix of the seven strategies. Here are the magnificent seven lead-generation strategies for trusted advisors, listed in descending order of effectiveness.

The Magnificent Seven

7. Showcase with workshops based on your proprietary research; support with telemarketing, direct mail, and publicity. This is the strategy of renting out the ballroom at the local Marriott or Hilton and charging for an all-day or half-day workshop. Participants should take away a substantial packet of good information from your firm (and a good meal too).

6. Publicity through the internet and social media. This is the water-drip torture school of marketing and the opposite of spam. By signing up for your e-newsletter lists, prospects tell you they are interested in what you have to say but not necessarily ready for a relationship now. These people should receive valuable how-to information and event invitations from you every month until they decide to opt out of the list. For social media, LinkedIn is best.

5. Networking and trade shows. This is an excellent way to gather business cards and ask permission to include them on your e-newsletter list. Focus on building your database.

4. Networking through community and association involvement. Everyone likes to do business with people they know, like, and trust. You need to get involved and "circulate to percolate," as some will say. Again, focus on building your database.

3. Publicity through publishing how-to articles in books and client-oriented press. Better than any brochure is the how-to article that appears in a publication that your target clients read. Books and blogs are ways to create buzz.

2. Showcase with how-to speeches and podcasts. People want to hire experts, and an expert, by definition, is someone who is invited to speak. Actively seek out forums to speak, and list past and future speaking dates on your website. Speak for a fee and speak for free, but target groups composed almost entirely of your great-fit and perfect-fit prospects.

1. Showcase with free or low-cost small-scale seminars, and support with telemarketing, direct mail, traditional publicity, and social media publicity. The best proactive tactic you can employ is regularly inviting prospects by mail and email to small seminars or group consultations. If your prospects are spread out geographically, you can do these briefings via webinars or seminars on Zoom. These can't be ninety-minute commercials. You need to present valuable information about how to solve your prospects' problems and then briefly mention your services.

Podcasting For Trusted Advisors

Why should a trusted advisor invest time in being a podcast guest or hosting a podcast?

In a word: networking.

Networking has always been a top way to attract right-fit clients, but podcasting and YouTube TV shows are a new spin on the strategy.

This works for all sorts of trusted advisors because it positions the trusted advisor as a subject matter expert.

A few years before the pandemic, ad agency owner Jodi Katz started her top-rated podcast, *Where Brains Meet Beauty*, to network within her industry in a way that felt rightsized for her personality.

"I've always been someone who feels really at ease one-on-one with new people, but I freeze when in a group," says Katz. "The bite-sized interview format of my show felt both safe and empowering to me as I explored a medium that was new to me."

Katz has been a respected voice in the beauty and wellness industry for almost twenty years, fifteen of them as founder and creative director of Base Beauty Creative Agency.

"The beauty of this medium is that you can set your own guard-rails," says Katz. "To celebrate our fifth anniversary, we innovated the remote format with live streaming—each episode is now recorded via YouTube Live, so our fans can watch the show get made in real time. For our classic podcast listeners, the episodes are still available for download in their favorite podcast apps."

Inviting guests to be on your TV show is way cooler than asking them to be on your podcast.

Katz started her career in advertising at the legendary agency BBDO, followed by positions on the editorial side of *Cosmopolitan* and *Glamour* magazines.

"I saw the podcast as a way to dig deeper and learn more about my peers than I could by quickly asking about their kids or their last job while rushing into a meeting or during chitchat at industry cocktail parties," says Katz. "I want to learn about my guests' childhood dreams, their motivations and goals, and how they feel about their journey so far."

To ensure that the wisdom of her guests reaches a wider audience, Katz asked me for editing help in writing a book based on the podcast Facing the Seduction of Success, published in 2022.[13] I asked Katz to share some tips for getting more success out of a podcast:

Listen to other shows in your genre. "My show is rooted in the beauty industry, and there are many podcasts devoted to beauty products, tips, and tricks," says Katz. "For my show to stand out, I needed a differentiating angle."

Think long term. "No matter your goal for a podcast, no success is reached overnight," adds Katz. "Think of this as an ongoing part of your workload, something that over a long time has the possibility to create real impact. But five or ten episodes won't get you there. Keep going, one step at a time, and momentum will come."

Recycle your podcast in many ways. "Be efficient with your time and resources by taking full advantage of your rich podcast content," says Katz. "Post transcripts of your shows on your website to feed Google rich SEO, use pull quotes from the show to reach new listeners via social media, make partnerships with like-minded industry events to promote their efforts while giving visibility to your show. Be creative here to work smarter, not harder."

Over two hundred episodes later, the show's role in her life goes way beyond networking.

Over two hundred episodes later, the show's role in her life goes way beyond networking.

"It's both free therapy and free business coaching for me, guided by the talented and ambitious guests that are generous with their time and vulnerability," says Katz.

Starting your own TV show/podcast is great, but don't forget you can be a guest on more than two million podcasts. The challenge is to be strategic.

First, understand who is your *who*. Then listen to podcasts that talk to your audience. Respectfully ask to be on the podcast by proving that you listen to the podcast. My suggestion is to target two appearances per month. Affordable services such as PodMatch can help you find podcasts that are right for you.

The Secrets Of Savvy Networking

Do you want to get high-paying clients? Then it would be best if you gave before you get when it comes to networking.

For advanced tips on networking, we went to the person who we think is the leading expert on the subject, author Susan RoAne. and she was generous enough to take the time to offer advice.

RoAne, aka the Mingling Maven, is a sought-after speaker and author of *How to Work a Room*, *The Secrets of Savvy Networking*, and more. She speaks for corporate, military, and university audiences. She has been featured in the *New York Times*, *Washington Post*, *Chicago Tribune*, *Wall Street Journal*, *San Francisco Chronicle*, and newspapers worldwide.

"One way to grow your networks is by joining organizations," says RoAne. "But joining any organization is merely step one in the process. The other steps can be implemented once you decide to grow your network, your circle of contacts, and your professional visibility."

RoAne also believes in the give-if-you-want-to-get philosophy. Don't just attend meetings and expect to reap benefits. There is more to networking than just showing up.

Here is RoAne's best advanced networking advice: get involved!

"Volunteer for the greeting committee and other projects," advises RoAne. "Then it's your job to greet, meet, and welcome everyone."

Once when I was president of a large advertising agency, I heard RoAne speak. Following her advice, I joined the San Diego Hotel Motel Association, and found out I was the only ad agency that joined ("Excellent," I said to myself in a Mr. Burns voice). I immediately signed up for the membership committee. I had three hotel accounts within a year because members saw me as a go-getter.

If you are willing to be a go-getter, RoAne has a three-step strategy to make volunteering pay:

Step One. "Get to know the leaders in the organization."

Step Two. "Extend yourself to other members and welcome their guests."

Step Three. "Throw your hat in the ring and run for office and give 120 percent if elected."

Following her advice to give 120 percent has meant that I have served as an officer for many groups, which required much volunteer time. But it has always paid off handsomely in attracting high-paying clients.

Another important RoAne tip is to be prepared when you attend functions. Visit websites, Google, LinkedIn, Facebook, and Instagram. Read a newspaper: in print, online, for a full banquet of conversation topics.

Also, draft your own self-introduction. It should be seven-to-nine seconds, not a thirty-second elevator speech. RoAne says there are several benefits to this approach:

Confidence. "When you know what you'll say about yourself, the more confident and comfortable you'll feel."

Name Awareness. "We teach people how to respond to us. If we introduce ourselves with our first and last names, over 80 percent of the time, people respond in kind. Then, we know each other's names."

Conversations. "When you give the benefit of what you do, you give people an opportunity to ask a question and begin the conversation."

RoAne says the magic is in the follow-up.
Do it within three to four days while
they still remember you.

RoAne says the magic is in the follow-up. Do it within three to four days while they still remember you. Reintroduce yourself by adding a comment referencing your conversation.

Networking To Find Clients With Clubhouse, Zoom, And LinkedIn

Networking ranks number five on my list of the top ten ways to attract high-paying clients. But the pandemic has left many wondering how networking makes sense these days.

The only four ways that rank higher on the list to attract high-paying clients are: hosting small-scale seminars, giving a speech at a client industry event, getting published with how-to articles in client industry publications, and doing volunteer work for client industry organizations (which is, in truth, a form of networking).

Before the pandemic, when trusted advisors could easily do business development at in-person meetings, networking at client industry events and trade shows was the best place to gather business cards and ask permission to be in touch.

But how did top trusted advisors keep making it rain during the shutdowns of the pandemic when in-person networking became problematic? The answer is that they pivoted and adapted.

Think of networking as a seed-planting activity. And as the scripture says: as you sow, so shall you reap. If someone is worth one seed, they are worth three seeds.

Here is an example of how one medical and pharma executive coach and consultant, Marieke Jonkman of New York, uses Clubhouse, Zoom, and LinkedIn to plant her three seeds with prospects.

Sample Of How Jonkman Plants First Seed On LinkedIn

Dear first name,

I first looked at your LinkedIn profile in 2017. That's when we connected on LinkedIn, and yet we've never "met."

Shame on us, right? To make things right, are you up for a virtual coffee over Zoom to share our mutual expertise and discuss current (and future?) topics in medical affairs/pharma? Shape the direction we are both going?

The purpose of the meeting would be:

1. How can we amplify each other?
2. Potential guest speaker on either Clubhouse or "Ask the MSL"?

Let me know if you're up to that! Send me some dates that work for you, or if it is easier for you, my calendar is available here:

 Please, no sales, dating, or informational interview calls, just networking!
Talk soon!
Warm regards,

Marieke Jonkman, PharmD, ACC, CEC, MHL
Medical Affairs Executive Coach

Sample Of How Jonkman Plants Second Seed On LinkedIn

Hi first name,

I was wondering if you had given some more thought about shaping the direction we both are going and see how we can inspire others to do the same?

So far, I've met with some great leaders around the globe and learned some epic things that I would have never guessed from just reading their LinkedIn page. And it has made our Clubhouse Club so much better and interesting.

The purpose of the meeting would be:

1. How can we amplify each other?
2. Potential guest speaker on either Clubhouse or "Ask the MSL"?

I hope I can persuade you as well, and if you do agree, please send me some dates/times that work for you, or if it's easier to just use my calendar that's fine too! I hope you're in!

PS No need for "swimming with sharks" stories.
PPS No sales, no dating, no informational interviews please.
Warm regards,

Marieke Jonkman, PharmD, ACC, CEC, MHL
Medical Affairs Executive Coach

Sample Of How Jonkman Plants Third Seed On LinkedIn

Hi first name,

Hey, it seems that networking is not the right thing for you now, but I still hope that you will join us sometime on Clubhouse!

Every Friday at noon EST we have a (lively) room to discuss current topics in medical affairs. You can find us @MedicalAffairs! I currently don't have any invites left for Clubhouse, but I can let you into the Medical Affairs Club, just send me a message!

I hope to see you there!

Warm regards,

Marieke Jonkman, PharmD, ACC, CEC, MHL
Medical Affairs Executive Coach

The Bottom Line. As one professional says, your net worth is determined by your network. Plant those seeds and expand your contacts through Clubhouse, Zoom, and LinkedIn.

How To Write Your Trusted Advisor Book In A Flash

For a trusted advisor, a book can be a secret weapon.

Imagine you are searching for a book on Amazon. After seeing the title and the book cover, you read the book's short description. Does it give you a great reason to read the book? Do you say to yourself, "The author understands me and my problem! I have to buy this book!"

Those are questions posed by trusted advisor Dan Janal, author of the book *Write Your Book in a Flash*.[14]

Janal has written more than a dozen books to help businesses build their brands. Six have been translated into other languages. He is an award-winning daily newspaper reporter and business newspaper editor. As a publicity and marketing expert, he has helped more than ten thousand authors and experts build their platforms over the past two decades with his highly regarded PR LEADS service.

After working with thousands of trusted advisors, he has seen a certain set of book genres. Janal suggests you might model one of these examples:

Legacy. Trusted advisors who want to leave their mark on the world and to help future generations will write memoirs. These books include tips for success and stories of overcoming obstacles. Suggested reading: *Basic Black: The Essential Guide for Getting Ahead at Work (and in Life)* by Cathie Black, first female publisher of *USA TODAY*. *Uncontainable: How Passion, Commitment, and Conscious Capitalism Built a Business Where Everyone Thrives* by Kip Tindell, founder of the Container Store.

Tools. Similar to legacy books, trusted advisors write these books to share ideas that brought them their success. Their motivations could be personal branding and helping others. Examples include *The Real-Life MBA* by Jack Welch and Suzy Welch or *The 4-Hour Workweek* by Timothy Ferriss.

Manifesto. Trusted advisors who are visionaries, have a certain point of view or want to change the world write these books. They want their readers to take up their causes. I've read manifestos on new ways of thinking about using the internet, customer service, and many other topics. Suggested reading: *Good to Great* by Jim Collins, *Thinking, Fast and Slow* by Daniel Kahneman, any book by Seth Godin, *Setting the Table: The Transforming Power of Hospitality in Business* by Danny Meyer, founder of Shake Shack. *Conscious Capitalism: Liberating the Heroic Spirit of Business* by John Mackey, co-founder of Whole Foods.

Proof. Trusted advisors present a hypothesis. They use case studies and statistics to prove their points. These authors—usually consultants at well-respected companies—want to establish their thought leadership. Suggested reading: *The Tipping Point* by Malcolm Gladwell. *Freakonomics* by Steven D. Levitt and Stephen J. Dubner.

How-To. Perhaps the most popular kind of book shows readers how to do something. Suggested reading: *How to Win Friends and Influence People* by Dale Carnegie. *Life Is Good: How to Live with Purpose and Enjoy the Ride* by Bert Jacobs and John Jacobs, founders of Life Is Good.

Process. These books offer research and show how to perform a task. Suggested reading: *Influence* by Robert B. Cialdini and *The Only Negotiating Guide You'll Ever Need* by Peter B. Stark and Jane Flaherty.

Training. These books are extensions of educational sessions. Suggested reading: *Loyal for Life* by John Tschohl.

Fictional. Also known as business fables, these books use fictional stories to show why certain business principles work. Suggested reading: *The Go-Giver* by Bob Burg and John David Mann and *Who Moved My Cheese?* by Spencer Johnson, MD.

Inspirational. Books offering motivational tips. Suggested reading: *Lifestorming* by Alan Weiss and Marshall Goldsmith.

"Your readers will buy your book if you write a great book summary," says Janal. "Best-selling authors start writing their books with the book description. This exercise helps you get focused and lets your ideal readers know immediately if they want to buy your book."

Why Your LinkedIn Is Not Attracting High-Paying Clients

If you want to use LinkedIn to attract high-paying clients, don't discuss how you will help. Be the rare, trusted advisor on the platform who just started helping.

That's the advice of the person who is arguably America's top LinkedIn thought leader, Ellen Melko Moore. She has consulted with the Oprah Winfrey Book Club and the Zappos guys and now teaches LinkedIn social selling strategies for some of the top thought leaders in the digital marketing space. She was a LinkedIn trainer of the year for the American Marketing Association.

"If you're looking to connect with ambitious, successful, high-fee B2B clients, LinkedIn is where you will find them," says Moore. "Mostly, they are not hanging out on Facebook or Instagram looking for real solutions to their business problems."

As for those important leaders who weren't using LinkedIn much before the quarantine adventures of 2020, they're active now.

"Anyone can make themselves look expert on other platforms, but only LinkedIn lets you see the whole history of that person's actual work," says Moore. "You can draw your own conclusions."

Here are four ways from Moore to up your LinkedIn game:

Slow down and focus on quality over quantity. Social media trends of the last decade have most experts convinced that digital marketing and sales are always about the numbers. Still, LinkedIn often works much better if professionals and consultants treat their LinkedIn network as a highly valuable asset. "In other words, slow down, go steady, and focus on the quality of your network rather than the quantity," says Moore. "Work on developing deeper relationships with the people who are best suited to be desirable clients or best placed to be powerful referral partners. We have one thought leader client with 150 connections, but every single one has real influence. He is killing it."

Redo your personal LinkedIn profile and make it for your target audience. "Instead of making your personal LinkedIn profile about you or your company, make it *for* your most important target audience, client, or partner," says Moore. "Think of your profile in a content marketing context vs. a promotional or historical context. The majority of professionals on LinkedIn—when they are ready to buy—are going to buy from the first person who gives them a significant shift in insight." So, don't waste your LinkedIn profile— especially the "About" section—talking about yourself or your company. Instead, focus on dropping those value bombs—so visitors to your profile can learn something important to *them*.

Stay away from automation and go easy on templates. Many trusted advisors want a "Done For Me" strategy on LinkedIn, which has given rise to multiple LinkedIn lead-generation companies that will help leaders craft templated messages and then use automation to send those messages, inviting hundreds of professionals daily to connect and communicate with that leader. "The only problem is that LinkedIn is cracking down on these companies, and using automation can get you kicked off the platform," says Moore. "LinkedIn really wants to emphasize their platform as a network, not a place to 'buy leads' on social media. Consider adopting this strategy instead: each day, find two to five high-quality people with whom you'd like to connect. Send a connection request that is personal and specific, vs. something that could be sent to thousands of people who resemble this person."

LinkedIn is a mystery to almost everyone on the platform. The pandemic boosted LInkedIn's popularity, with 660 million users at the start of 2021. "More importantly, 55 percent of decision-makers use LinkedIn content to choose the organizations with whom they want to work," says Moore. "And one in five investors say it's the best place to learn about a topic. But despite LinkedIn's growing popularity, it's hard to find people who express confidence in using the platform for professional or business development. Many thought leaders who are powerful and popular in other mediums aren't sure how to handle LinkedIn."

The bottom line: All this is good news for those trusted advisors who choose to optimize LinkedIn. It means you have a real chance of making progress quickly if you put in some attention and intention and practice offering help, not hype.

8

☸

Feed The Funnel Is Star Six

The eternal stars shine out again,
so soon as it is dark enough.

Thomas Carlyle

Think of a funnel as the entry point to your business development pipeline.

A business development pipeline is an organized way of tracking multiple potential prospects as they progress through different stages of becoming a client.

Most trusted advisors hesitate to invest in business development and coaching. But when you're clear on your client lifetime value (CLV), you'll feel more confident and excited to invest 10 percent, 15 percent, or even 25 percent or more into building a robust pipeline of qualified prospects.

If you question the 25 percent number, think of it this way. If someone was willing to give you a $100 bill and all they asked in return was $25, how long would you be ready to make those exchanges? Now there is an image to conjure up in your mind's eye.

Because human brains are hardwired to think in images, not words, pipelines are often visualized as a horizontal bar, sometimes as a funnel, divided into the stages of attracting a new client. You invest in business development to feed the funnel of your pipeline.

Do you think business development for a consultant is an expense or an investment? Your answer can have huge ramifications for attracting high-paying clients.

Many people, including your competitors, try to spend as little as possible on feeding their funnel because they view it as an expense.

But a little arithmetic might change your mind.

"When you shift your mindset to seeing it as an investment, you open up a new world of possibilities," says Michael Zipursky.

Zipursky is the CEO of Consulting Success and the author of the book *Act Now*.[15] He has advised organizations like Financial Times, Dow Jones, RBC, and helped Panasonic launch new products into global markets.

"You can invest into more and better marketing, find new ways to create and deliver value for your ideal clients, and create an experience that they want to be part of," says Zipursky. "In a study we did, we found that people who invest more into their marketing have higher revenue and incomes than those that spend less on marketing."

Does the thought of spending thousands of dollars on feeding the funnel excite you?

"If you're like most business owners, you shudder at the thought of spending anything on marketing," says Zipursky. "However, this mindset is holding you back from attracting high-value clients, creating an advantage over your competition—and ultimately, winning more business."

The problem is that you're treating marketing like an expense instead of an investment.

The best way to change your mindset is to understand your client's lifetime value, commonly expressed by the initials CLV.

Here's a three-step exercise to figure out your CLV:

Step One. Calculate how much a client spends with you on an average engagement/project. Example: Your clients pay you $5,000 on a monthly retainer.

Step Two. Determine how long a client typically works with you. Example: You typically work with a client for 18 months.

Step Three. Multiply your average engagement value by the amount of time you work with your client. Example: $5,000 x 18 = $90,000.

Over their lifetime, clients like this are worth $90,000 to your business. That's your CLV.

Use your project's average price if you don't charge a monthly fee. Then, multiply it by how many times the client invests that amount to work with you over two years or longer if they typically stay longer.

The next calculation is to determine how much you are currently spending on business development. Be honest, don't include those expenses you hide in marketing, like client entertainment and tickets to sporting events.

Business development is what you do to get the attention and interest of your ideal clients, so they want to have a conversation with you.

"If you know that your CLV is $90,000, how much are you open to investing in attracting and winning a new client?" asks Zipursky. The key word is *invest.*

How much are you currently putting toward feeding your funnel? Knowing your CLV puts into perspective how much you can actually invest in your business development.

Feeding The Funnel Is Enrollment

Offering a great service is not good enough. You must learn the subtle art of feeding the funnel through enrollment conversations.

"Trusted advisors tell me they don't want to think of themself as a salesperson," says business development expert David Goldman, author of the book *The Road to Happiness*[16] and coauthor of the book *Bringing in the Business*.[17] "You may want to grow your business, increase your client base, and actually sell more services. But sales is an unwelcome concept."

Finding high-paying clients is really an enrollment process.

Finding high-paying clients is really an enrollment process. But what do you say to enroll prospects?

"At your best, a trusted advisor enrolls a prospect into the possibility that their service is for them," says Goldman.

Goldman has helped attorneys, financial advisors, and other trusted advisors double revenues through a simple five-step enrollment process:

Step One. There must be some background of relationship. "Some rapport must be established," says Goldman. "This doesn't have to be elaborate, nor does it have to take a great deal of time to do. Without it, however, nothing will go further. It could be an introduction or a referral from someone else. It could be meeting someone at a function or a business gathering. It could even be from a completely unknown source. But there must be a relationship. You can establish this with a simple question. Ask, 'What was it that had you want to meet with me today?' Then listen. That will be enough to establish that there is a relationship."

Step Two. A conversation for possibility, the most important part of the process. "The entire deal hinges on this piece," says Goldman. "Once there is a relationship, *possibility* is the most important part of the process. The conversation for possibility is simply establishing the possibility that your product or service could be for the client or prospect. This is where the entire reason for your service is brought to light, in complete detail. In fact, the more said about the possibility of your offering, the better. Here's the catch: The conversation for possibility must come from the client's or prospect's mouth. So, you must ask the kinds of questions that elicit the appropriate response from the other person."

Step Three. A conversation for value. "As with the conversation for possibility, the conversation for value must also come from the prospect or client," says Goldman. "You say, 'Let's suppose that I can help you make all of the things on your list happen. What would that value be, in real terms, in your life?' Be prepared for them to say, 'I don't know.' Do not accept that answer. Simply say, 'I realize that it's not an easy question. However, take a look. What would it be worth to you?'" Be prepared for fuzzy, vague, general answers. You must stay focused on getting a real number that represents what the prospect thinks the value of your product or service would be.

Step Four. A conversation for opportunity. "Now you get to talk about your program or service," says Goldman. "You can tailor what you have to say based on what the client is looking for. This is not meant to be manipulative in any way. If your service is not what the client is looking for, simply say so and refer someone else to the client and move on. Explain how your service works. Don't overdo it. Remember, less is more."

Step Five. The call to action. "No matter how smoothly the rest of the process goes, you still must ask for the business," says Goldman.

"I say: 'I only have one close, and I usually tell you when it's coming—pretty soon. First, do you have any questions?' Answer any questions they might have. My favorite closing question is, 'On a scale of one to ten, where one means you never want to see me again and ten means you are ready to start tomorrow, where are you? What will it take to get to ten?'"

Goldman says you could also simply ask, "Does this make sense? Are you ready to proceed?" Or, "Here's the next step; when do you want to start?"

Goldman's main message is that no prospect wants to be sold, but many would enjoy being enrolled.

Yes, Some Math Is Involved

Think of feeding the funnel as everything you do to get a prospect to have a meaningful conversation about retaining you. Once that conversation has been held, what has to happen next in your world to move through the pipeline?

For some trusted advisors, one conversation is all they need for the prospect to decide. In our interviews with trusted advisors for this book, one trusted advisor in the payroll/accounting world said it took six separate steps for a prospect to move through the pipeline.

Feeding the funnel is about ensuring your opportunity pipeline is full from top to bottom with qualified prospects.

Feeding the funnel is about ensuring your opportunity pipeline is full from top to bottom with qualified prospects.

Feeding the funnel is about generating leads that come into the opportunity pipeline. A proper pipeline helps you keep track of the prospects so they don't fall through the cracks (or so as not to mix metaphors, leak out of your pipeline and evaporate). Trusting the names to your mental pipeline is a poor decision for a busy trusted advisor.

Busy trusted advisors still need to find time to do regular funnel math. Use a worksheet to calculate the inputs and outputs needed for your opportunity funnel. For your revenue goal, how many leads do you need to generate? What is your close ratio (aka batting average)? What is the average deal size in dollars? This is not calculus; this is basic arithmetic.

The purpose of all this math is to control what you can control. You cannot control results, like who decides to become a client (prospects have their reasons for doing what they do). You cannot substantially change your close ratio (however, all trusted advisors could benefit from training on improving their batting average through questioning and active listening).

What you can control is feeding the funnel through lead generation. In California, we tell trusted advisors that the Universe rewards activity; in the Midwest, we say the Lord helps those who help themselves. We are bilingual.

Ratios Don't Change Much

When coauthor Henry DeVries was a vice president for business development for a $5 billion international financial services firm, he had a problem. Revenue numbers were in steady decline. Henry researched the pipeline math and found the following ratio held true for his trusted advisors:

Attraction phase conversations with qualified prospects	10
Appointments booked for meaningful conversation	4
Appointments kept for meaningful conversation	2
High-paying clients signed	1

So, the 10:4:2:1 ratio was consistent. Through extensive training, Henry tried to improve the appointments kept to clients signed ratio, but nothing affected that ratio. Then, he worked on improving the appointments booked to appointments kept ratio. Nothing moved the needle.

But he discovered he could control the quantity of attraction phase conversations with qualified prospects, or in other words, feeding the funnel. This is what he could control, and this is what he invested in. Two particular lead-generation programs increased the number of qualified prospects entering the funnel and dropping to the bottom line. The next challenge was recruiting more trusted advisors to handle the increase in qualified leads.

8

Funnel Math Worksheet

The whole idea behind this is based on who I am as a trusted advisor. If I can plug in the input numbers, it will tell me how much activity you need to generate to make your desired numbers. The numbers you shoot for can be top-line revenue or what you take home as gross income. This takes a little more math.

	Monthly	Weekly (48 work weeks)	Daily	Quarterly (240 work days)	Annually
Target Revenue	$10,000	$2,500	$500	$30,000	$120,000
Average Revenue/ Sale	$2,500	$2,500	$2,500	$2,500	$2,500
# Sales to Reach Target Revenue	4.00	1.00	0.20	12.00	48.00
Opportunity to Close Ratio	30.0%	30.0%	30.0%	30.0%	30.0%
# Opportunities to Reach Target Revenue	13.33	3.33	0.67	40.00	160.00
# Business Development Meetings to Reach Target Revenue	40.00	10.00	2.00	120.00	480.00
# Business Development Meetings Needed to Close an Opportunity	3	3	3	3	3
# Prospecting Calls Needed to Identify an Opportunity	10	10	10	10	10
Average # of Opportunities per Account	2	2	2	2	2
# Prospecting Calls	200	50	10	600	2,400

PART III

Staying The Course

9

Keep Your Stars Aligned

I like the night. Without the dark, we'd never see the stars.

Stephenie Meyer, in *Twilight*

The biggest business development mystery for trusted advisors is how to keep their stars aligned.

That means attracting high-paying clients on a regular and consistent basis.

Clients want to hire the authority in the field. The key is to be a thought leader who is sought and bought, not just another professional who has to continually tell and sell to find clients.

When a trusted advisor can become a trusted authority, feeding the funnel becomes so much easier.

When a trusted advisor can become a trusted authority, feeding the funnel becomes so much easier.

The research results in this book prove there is a better way. There is a proven process for business development with integrity that generates a 400 percent to 2,000 percent return on your investment. Call it the Marketing With Authority Model, and the most successful trusted advisors use it to attract more high-paying clients than they can handle.

If you struggle to keep your pipeline filled with qualified prospects, you are not alone. Management expert Peter Drucker once wrote, "There is only one valid definition of business purpose: to create a customer." To do this, a business must answer three classic questions: What is our business? Who is our client? What does our client consider valuable?[18]

All businesses struggle with this, especially trusted advisors who are independent consultants and solo professionals.

To attract new clients, the best approach is to position your expertise. Be a thought leader who demonstrates expertise by "giving away" valuable information through writing and speaking.

Science backs this up. Ten years of research with thousands of trusted advisors demonstrates they can fill a pipeline with qualified prospects in as little as thirty days by advising prospects on overcoming their most pressing problems.[19]

The Marketing With Authority Model In Action

Does the Marketing With Authority Model really work, or is this just for ultra-gifted virtuosos? Here are just a few concrete examples:

- Through an informational website and electronic newsletter, one trusted advisor added an additional $100,000 in annual revenue from speaking engagements and sales of information products within two years.

- In forty-five days, one trusted advisor serving the home building industry launched a website and thought leadership campaign that helped him double his revenues in a year.

- Using the speaking strategy alone, a web marketing trusted advisor doubled his income and added $100,000 of revenue in one year.

- By switching to the Thought Leader Model, a marketing services firm of trusted advisors received a 2,000 percent return on investment from its new business development campaign that featured how-to advice seminars and articles from senior executives.

- When a trusted advisor IT consultant gave up cold calling and switched to the model, the quality of his leads dramatically improved, and closed deals quickly increased by 25 percent.

- Through getting published and public speaking, a group of trusted advisor labor lawyers has grown from a regional practice to a national firm in a few years.

- A well-established regional accounting firm reported they were able to accomplish more business development in six months with the model than they had in three years on their own.

- An advertising agency used the strategy to double revenues from $4.5 to $9.6 million in five years and earn a spot in the Ad Age 500.

Invest In Being Guided By The Stars

What should you do to increase revenues by being a thought leader? First, understand that generating prospects is an investment and should be measured like any other investment.

Rather than creating a brochure, start by writing how-to articles. Those articles turn into speeches, seminars, and podcasts. Eventually, you gather the articles and publish a book through a strategy called print-on-demand independent publishing. Does it work? Here is a list of three business best-seller titles by consultants that started out independently published:[20]

The One Minute Manager, by Kenneth Blanchard and Spencer Johnson: picked up by William Morrow & Co. and proceeded to sell twelve million copies.

In Search of Excellence, by Thomas J. Peters (of McKinsey & Co.): in its first year, sold more than 25,000 copies directly to consumers—then Warner sold ten million more.

Leadership Secrets of Attila the Hun, by Wess Roberts, sold half a million copies before being picked up by Warner.

Overall, quit wasting money on ineffective means like brochures, advertising, and sponsorships. The best business development investment trusted advisors can make is to create informative websites, host persuasive seminars, book speaking engagements, and get published as a columnist and eventually as the author of a book. Your goal should be to become one of the most sought-after authorities in your field.

What Is My North Star?

If you are a trusted advisor who wants more impact and influence, where should you invest your time, talent, and treasure? What is your North Star that should guide you?

The clear-cut answer: regularly host small-scale seminars for five to ten prospects.

In the last five years, we have interviewed hundreds of trusted advisors who have built their businesses this way. Here are examples:

An Indiana sales consultant used seminars and publishing books to set himself apart from the competition and build a multimillion-dollar consulting firm. He finds riches in the niche of clients wanting to land the big whale accounts.

A Tennessee dental practice consultant makes more than $280,000 annually as a speaker and consultant. For over twenty years, she had wanted to put on seminars and write a book, but it was more of a wish than anything until she took the time to learn how to do it.

A California hiring and executive search practice firm used the seminar strategy to add at least $250,000 per year in additional revenue for the past decade. The firm's seminars reveal the big blunder that causes more than half of recruited executives to fail to meet expectations in the first eighteen months.

Even successful, trusted advisors say business development is a grind. They say their main problem is not enough credibility, not enough influence, and not enough new clients on a sustainable basis. Yes, even trusted advisors who are doing well can wake up anxious. However, research has proven there is a better way. This problem can be solved in three steps.

Step One. Pick the pain. Are you into pain? If you want high-paying clients, you should be. Select a target-rich audience that consists of prospects who need your services. Then determine what pain they want solved that you can help with. Choose a title for the event. One good approach is to offer to help them overcome common blunders in this area.

Step Two. Pick a place, date, and time. In the former times before the pandemic, the most choices for locations were conference rooms in large law and accounting offices, banks, chambers of commerce, country clubs, colleges, and hotels (the most expensive option). After COVID-19 hit, the most common location was Zoom. A new word was coined, Zoominar. Moving forward, expect a combination of live and virtual events.

Step Three. Pick the right content. There's too much information out there. What prospects want is analysis. Don't bombard attendees with 1,001 ways to solve the problem; give them the seven best solutions. Make the sessions. Offer follow-up one-on-one strategy calls.

How To Improve Business Development With Zoominars

Not to be an alarmist, but many trusted advisors are testing positive for Zoom fatigue.

Well, get over it. Zoom is your new best friend when it comes to business development.

Perhaps time and distance are keeping you and your prospects apart. If you serve clients who are located throughout the country or even in different countries, the pandemic has actually had a benefit. The silver lining to the cloud is the widespread adoption of Zoom.

This has given rise to the Zoominar, a virtual seminar that allows you to host inexpensive meetings for people from anywhere.

While generating high-paying clients through small-scale seminars is a proven marketing strategy for consultants and professionals, times have been tough. Many professionals and consultants are frustrated that you can't gather prospects into a room like you used to. Others are frustrated by a lack of turnout for the Zoominars they do host.

Here are our top ten recommendations to increase attendance for your next lead-generation event on Zoom:

1. **Develop a checklist and timeline of your pre- and post-Zoominar activities.**

2. **Determine your target audience of prospects.** LinkedIn is a great tool to find people if you know details about them (we entered all that info about ourselves in LinkedIn, and it is searchable).

3. **Use informal research to pretest the potential topics to make sure the one you choose has the most appeal to your target audience.** A great option is always: "The Three Biggest Blunders _____ Make When Doing _____."

4. **Make sure emails, social media postings, web landing pages, and LinkedIn messages convey a first-class image for you.**

5. **Confirm registrations forty-eight hours before the event by email.** If you want to be a business development champion, reach out and call prospects to tell them you are looking forward to meeting them and ask if they have any specific questions they want you to cover.

6. **Deliver seminar content that is of real value.** Make it a no-selling zone. Delivering a thinly disguised sales pitch is the kiss of death.

7. **Make it easy for the prospect to have a strategy call later on.** Offer this briefly during the seminar and send the follow-up offer by email. Make it clear it is a no-selling call and honor that.

8. **For the strategy call, the recommended agenda is to get clarity around their goals, assets, and roadblocks and to learn from you how others have gotten from where they are to where they want to go.**

9. **Conduct organized follow-up to stay in touch with the people who signed up to attend but did not make it.** These are the forgotten few. They are interested in the topic, but something came up, and the easiest item on the day to say no to is the Zoominar. About 50 percent who sign up do not show up, and they are still great prospects.

10. **Measure, measure, measure.** Be sure to measure all aspects of the program to see what could be improved. Measure how many were invited, how many accepted, how many attended, how many who attended booked a strategy call, how many kept the call, and how many of those callers became clients.

The number one challenge for trusted advisors is creating new clients. Zoominars are a dignified way to network with prospects and develop new referral sources.

10

Into Your Future

The nitrogen in our DNA, the calcium in our teeth, the iron in our blood, the carbon in our apple pies were made in the interiors of collapsing stars. We are made of starstuff.

Carl Sagan, in *Cosmos*

Here is a quick recap of the NavSTAR Client Acquisition System:

Star One. Targeting. The first proactive step is to know who you want. Avoid the poetic approach of Henry Wadsworth Longfellow: "I shot an arrow into the air. It fell to earth, I knew not where."

Star Two. Messaging. When you find your *who*, use a message that is right for them. Test, test, and test your messages some more.

Star Three. Biz dev process. Map your process and eliminate any wasteful steps. The journey is just too important to wing it.

Star Four. Biz dev success scorecard. What gets measured gets managed. Determine your metrics and measure them.

Star Five. Lead generation. Generating a prospective lead is like getting an at bat in baseball. You cannot get a hit if you don't have an at bat. Share your expertise through speaking, talking, and networking.

Star Six. Feed the funnel. Like the shampoo bottle says: lather, rinse, repeat. The funnel is the entrance to your pipeline of qualified prospects who have a problem you can help solve and a budget to solve the problem.

And In Closing

We close with a quote from the seminal book on business development, the 1909 classic *The Science of Getting Rich* by Wallace D. Wattles.[21]

> *The men and women who practice the foregoing instructions will certainly get rich; and the riches they receive will be in exact proportion to the definiteness of their vision, the fixity of their purpose, the steadiness of their faith, and the depth of their gratitude.*

The riches for trusted advisors are a steady and predictable stream of right-fit clients. You now have the stars to guide you. As the mariners of days gone by would say, we wish you plain sailing for your journey ahead.

Appendix

A   Strategy Recap

As the stars guide you, here are a few strategies to help you on your journey. We wish you the best.

NavSTAR Client Acquisition System Strategy #1
The "Circus Is Coming To Town" strategy: Showcase your knowledge by staging small-scale seminars. Take the show on the road to various cities. When you are just passing through, prospects must decide whether to engage or not.

NavSTAR Client Acquisition System Strategy #2
The "Pause Three Seconds For Dignity" strategy: When a prospect, meeting planner, or journalist asks you a good question—such as would you like to speak for us or are you available to take on new clients—pause three seconds for dignity and calmly say "Thank you for asking."

NavSTAR Client Acquisition System Strategy #3
The "Book Is The Starting Line" strategy: A book is the number one marketing tool, and a speech is the number one marketing strategy

for trusted advisors to attract high-paying clients. A book is the best business card/brochure a trusted advisor could ever produce. The right book can be an asset to every trusted advisor on the team.

NavSTAR Client Acquisition System Strategy #4

The "Humans Are Hardwired For Stories" strategy: Tell stories in your presentations, speeches, articles, and books about clients you have helped take from a mess to a success. The client is the main character, and you are the mentor character.

NavSTAR Client Acquisition System Strategy #5

The "Happy New Year" strategy: Reset your counters to zero every thirty days. Track your numbers every month. You get to celebrate a happy new year every first of the month.

NavSTAR Client Acquisition System Strategy #6

The "Consistency Trumps Commitment" strategy: Approach business development with purpose. What you do daily is more important than what you do occasionally. Establish standards, benchmarks, and milestones for your business development.

NavSTAR Client Acquisition System Strategy #7

The "Magic Is In The Mix" strategy: In marketing, the magic is in the work. No one strategy works for everyone. Use at least five different lead-generation strategies.

NavSTAR Client Acquisition System Strategy #8

The "People Buy From People" strategy: Even if there are twenty on the team, each trusted advisor must first sell themselves, not the firm. People do business with people they know, like, and trust.

NavSTAR Client Acquisition System Strategy #9

The "Book, Speech, Website Trifecta" strategy: The title of your book, the title of your speech, and the website domain should be the same. Each book is its own brand. A trusted authority has more than one book.

NavSTAR Client Acquisition System Strategy #10

The "If You Would Be Open" strategy: Start all your asks with the phrase "If you would be open…." If is a magic word, it is a soft knock at the door. For example: "If you would be open to a conversation about booking me as a speaker, that would be great."

NavSTAR Client Acquisition System Strategy #11

The "I Wish I Could" strategy. Never say no to a prospect. Saying no hurts rapport. Instead say, "I wish I could."

NavSTAR Client Acquisition System Strategy #12

The "Listen Carefully" strategy. This is from the author and our great friend, Mark LeBlanc. Sometimes you need to listen carefully and respond appropriately. We say, other times, you need to listen carefully and keep your mouth shut.

NavSTAR Client Acquisition System Strategy #13

This is the "Pain Into Gain Riddle" strategy. Your target prospects experience their unique frustrations and pains. As the old adage states, "People don't care what you know, until they know that you care." Truly identifying your prospect's predicament tells them you understand and empathize with them.

NavSTAR Client Acquisition System Strategy #14

The "Offer Advice In General" strategy. Research shows trusted advisors can fill a pipeline with qualified clients in as little as thirty days by offering prospects advice on overcoming pressing problems, if they have the right marketing DNA.

NavSTAR Client Acquisition System Strategy #15

The "Collect Measurement-Based Testimonials" strategy. Prospects want to hear about real numbers like dollars earned or saved, percentages of improvements, and time-based measures of how quickly results were achieved.

NavSTAR Client Acquisition System Strategy #16

The "Plant Three Seeds A Day" strategy: There is a universal truth that as you sow, so shall you reap. A trusted advisor should plant at least three seeds each and every day to attract clients.

SPEED YOUR PROGRESS WITH THE
NavSTAR Client Acquisition^{SM} Toolkit

Want to Take Your Client Acquisition to the Next Level?

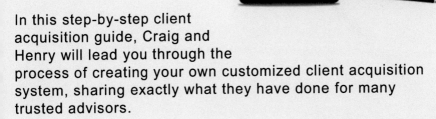

Now that you've finished *Trusted Advisor Confidential*, it's time to go deeper with templates and worksheets.

In this step-by-step client acquisition guide, Craig and Henry will lead you through the process of creating your own customized client acquisition system, sharing exactly what they have done for many trusted advisors.

With the *NavSTAR Client Acquisition System Toolkit*, you'll learn everything you need to know to generate a significant, predicatable, and sustainable book of business.

Are You Ready To Align Your Client Acquisition Stars?

C   Acknowledgments

Craig Lowder. I am humbled and grateful to have completed my latest book *Trusted Advisor Confidential*. This project has been both a labor of love and a source of pain. Nevertheless, it has been a rewarding journey that I hope will empower you, the reader, to achieve your professional and personal aspirations.

First, I want to express my gratitude to my Lord and Savior, Jesus Christ, for guiding me on my life journey of learning and sharing. Without His grace and blessings, this book would not have been possible.

I want to acknowledge my family for their unwavering love and support throughout this voyage. To my wife Peggy, daughters Erin and Shanon, our sons-in-law Chris and Dave, and our granddaughters Jazz and Chloe thank you for your patience and understanding. Your encouragement and motivation have been the foundation of my success.

I am deeply indebted to my coauthor and publisher, Henry DeVries. Henry, you were my guide star, inspiration, and taskmaster (as needed) in bringing this book to life. Your patience, understanding, and guidance have been invaluable. I am honored to be your wingman.

I would also like to extend my sincere gratitude to my clients and fellow trusted advisors. Thank you for sharing your experiences and stories with me, allowing me to lend legitimacy to the thoughts shared in this book. Your trust and confidence have been the cornerstone of my professional growth.

Last, I want to thank the readers of this book. It is my sincere hope that the ideas expressed within will empower you to build a robust book of business and fulfill your life dreams. I am honored to have shared this journey with you.

Thank you.

Henry DeVries. I wish to express gratitude for my many mentors who have recently passed: professor Glen Broom of San Diego State University, the world's leading public relations scholar, for four decades of mentoring and friendship; *Chino Valley Champion* newspaper publisher Al McCombs, who gave me, at the age of fifteen, my first paying job as a writer; my first coauthor Diane Gage Lofgren, who in 1990 taught me to be a coauthor; and professor Jack Douglass of UC San Diego, who in 1975 gladly took this teenager straight off a farm under his wing and taught me how to create the career of my dreams.

Thanks to all those who agreed to be interviewed to share their advice on business development in my weekly column for Forbes.com.

Also, I want to thank the team at Indie Books International, including Mark LeBlanc, Ann LeBlanc, Vikki DeVries, Devin DeVries, Suzanne Hagen, Joni McPherson, Denise Montgomery, Jack DeVries, Don Sevrens, Sally Romoser, Heather Pendley, Taylor Graham, Adrienne Moch, Eric Gudas, Lisa Lucas, Gail Sevrens, Jordan DeVries, Bill Ramsey, Steve Plummer, and so many others who have helped me create my masterpiece: a business that is the Apple Computer of consultant books, making it easy and affordable for every consultant to have more credibility, more impact, and more influence. To my Heavenly Father, thank you for helping me expand my territory so I can serve more of your children to get what they want in life. Thank you to the hundreds of authors, vendors, and investors who chose Indie Books International.

D   About The Authors

Craig Lowder, MBA, is a sales effectiveness and lead-conversion expert with over thirty years of experience helping trusted advisors and small- to midsized business owners achieve remarkable growth in their top-line revenues and personal incomes. With an impressive track record of success, Craig is widely recognized for his ability to empower his clients to achieve significant and predictable sales growth year after year.

Craig is the creator of the trademarked Star Guide and Nav-STAR Client Acquisition systems, proven approaches to sales and business development that have helped countless individuals and organizations achieve exceptional results. Through his unique blend of strategic thinking, practical insights, and hands-on guidance, Craig has become a trusted advisor to many of his clients, helping them navigate complex challenges and achieve their most ambitious goals.

Over the course of his career, Craig has worked with clients in a wide range of industries, including manufacturing, wholesale distribution, finance, business service, technology, and more. He has helped individuals and organizations of all sizes optimize their sales processes, improve lead-conversion rates, and build stronger, more profitable businesses.

Beyond his work as a sales effectiveness and lead-conversion expert, Craig is also a sought-after speaker and thought leader in his field. He is a frequent contributor to industry publications and has been featured in a variety of media outlets.

Whether working one-on-one with clients or speaking to large audiences, Craig is passionate about sharing his knowledge and insights to help others achieve success. With his proven track record of success, deep expertise, and unwavering commitment to his client's success, Craig Lowder is truly one of the most respected and accomplished sales effectiveness and lead-conversion experts in the business today. Learn more about Craig at his LinkedIn page: https://www.linkedin.com/in/craiglowder/ or by visiting his website at CraigLowder.com

Other Books by Craig Lowder:

Smooth Selling Forever

Henry DeVries, MBA, writes a weekly business development column for Forbes.com and is the cohost of *The Marketing With A Book Podcast.* He is CEO of Indie Books International and has ghostwritten or edited more than 300 business books, including his #1 Amazon sales and marketing bestseller, *How to Close a Deal Like Warren Buffett.* In his book and presentations titled *"Persuade with a Story!"* he shows thousands of professionals each year how to uncover hidden asset hero stories that communicate trustworthiness in two minutes or less. He earned his MBA from San Diego State University and a certificate in Leading Professional Service Firms from the Harvard Business School. On a personal note, he is a baseball nut who has visited forty-four major league baseball parks and has three to go before he can touch 'em all. He can be reached at henry@indiebooksintl.com. Learn more about Henry at his LinkedIn page: https://www.linkedin.com/in/henryjdevries/ or by visiting the website for Indie Books International: IndieBooksIntl.com.

Other Books by Henry DeVries:

Self-Marketing Secrets (with Diane Gage)

Pain-Killer Marketing (with Chris Stiehl)

Client Seduction (with Denise Bryson)

Closing America's Job Gap (with Mary Walshok and Tapan Munroe)

Marketing the Marketers

How to Close a Deal Like Warren Buffett (with Tom Searcy)

Marketing with a Book

Persuade with a Story!

Client Attraction Chain Reaction

Build Your Consulting Practice (with Mark LeBlanc)

Defining You (with Mark LeBlanc and Kathy McAfee)

Persuade with a Case Acceptance Story! (with Penny Reed and Mark LeBlanc)

Persuade with a Digital Content Story! (with Lisa Apolinski)

Rainmaker Confidential (with Scott Love and Mark LeBlanc)

Bringing in the Business (with David Goldman and Mark LeBlanc)

Marketing with a Book for Agency Owners

24 Ways to Get Paid to Speak (with Nona Prather)

E   Works Referenced And Notes

1. David Maister, *Managing the Professional Service Firm* (New York: Free Press, 1993).

2. Henry DeVries, *Marketing With A Book: The Science of Attracting High-Paying Clients for Consultants and Coaches* (Oceanside, CA: Indie Books International, 2015).

3. Margaret Reynolds, *Reignite: How Everyday Companies Spark Next-Stage Growth* (Oceanside, CA: Indie Books International, 2015).

4. Margaret Reynolds, *Boost Your GrowthDNA* (Oceanside, CA: Indie Books International, 2019).

5. Erik Peterson and Tim Riesterer, *Conversations That Win the Complex Sale* (New York: McGraw Hill, 2011).

6. Peterson and Riesterer, *Conversations.*

7. Henry DeVries, "The Greatest Business Branding Strategy In The World," Forbes.com, August 10, 2018, https://www.forbes.com/sites/henrydevries/2018/08/10/the-greatest-business-branding-strategy-in-the-world/

8. Bryan Gray, Jesse Laffen, et al., *The Priority Sale: How To Connect Your Real Impact To Your Prospects' Top Priorities* (Oceanside, CA: Indie Books International, 2021).

9. Peterson and Riesterer, *Conversations.*

10. Lisa Rehurek, *Dare To Be Influential*, (Oceanside, CA: Indie Books International, 2020).

11. Eli Schwartz, *Product-Led SEO: The Why Behind Building Your Organic Growth Strategy* (Fayetteville, AR: Houndstooth Press, 2021).

12. James Ware, *Making Meetings Matter: How Smart Leaders Orchestrate Powerful Conversations in the Digital Age* (Oceanside, CA: Indie Books International, 2016).

13. Jodi Katz, *Facing the Seduction of Success: Inspiring Stories of Leading in Business While Living Your Life* (Oceanside, CA: Indie Books International, 2022).

14. Dan Janal, *Write Your Book in a Flash: The Paint-by-Numbers System to Write the Book of Your Dreams—FAST!* (Granger, IN: TCK Publishing, 2018).

15. Michael Zipursky, *Act Now: How Successful Consultants Thrive during Chaos and Uncertainty* (East Sussex: Consulting Success, 2020).

16. David Goldman, *The Road to Happiness: How to Get What You Really Want* (Oceanside, CA: Indie Books International, 2019).

17. David Goldman, Mark LeBlanc, and Henry DeVries, *Bringing in the Business* (Oceanside, CA: Indie Books International, 2023).

18. Peter F. Drucker, *The Practice of Management* (New York: Harper & Row, 1954).

19. Henry DeVries and Denise Bryson, *Client Seduction* (Bloomington, IN: AuthorHouse, 2005).

20. Southwest Airlines, *Spirit*, March 2005.

21. Wallace D. Wattles, *The Science of Getting Rich* (New York: Elizabeth Towne Publishing, 1909).

F   Index

Made in the USA
Monee, IL
28 January 2024